Longitudinal Surveys of Children

Kirsten K. West, Robert M. Hauser, and Terri M. Scanlan, Editors

Committee on National Statistics
Board on Children, Youth, and Families

Commission on Behavioral and Social Sciences and Education

National Research Council | Institute of Medicine

NATIONAL ACADEMY PRESS
Washington, D.C. 1998

NATIONAL ACADEMY PRESS   2101 Constitution Avenue, N.W.   Washington, D.C. 20418

NOTICE: The project that is the subject of this report was approved by the Governing Board of the National Research Council, whose members are drawn from the councils of the National Academy of Sciences, the National Academy of Engineering, and the Institute of Medicine. The members of the committee responsible for the report were chosen for their special competences and with regard for appropriate balance.

The National Academy of Sciences is a private, nonprofit, self-perpetuating society of distinguished scholars engaged in scientific and engineering research, dedicated to the furtherance of science and technology and to their use for the general welfare. Upon the authority of the charter granted to it by the Congress in 1863, the Academy has a mandate that requires it to advise the federal government on scientific and technical matters. Dr. Bruce M. Alberts is president of the National Academy of Sciences.

The National Academy of Engineering was established in 1964, under the charter of the National Academy of Sciences, as a parallel organization of outstanding engineers. It is autonomous in its administration and in the selection of its members, sharing with the National Academy of Sciences the responsibility for advising the federal government. The National Academy of Engineering also sponsors engineering programs aimed at meeting national needs, encourages education and research, and recognizes the superior achievements of engineers. Dr. William A. Wulf is president of the National Academy of Engineering.

The Institute of Medicine was established in 1970 by the National Academy of Sciences to secure the services of eminent members of appropriate professions in the examination of policy matters pertaining to the health of the public. The Institute acts under the responsibility given to the National Academy of Sciences by its congressional charter to be an adviser to the federal government and, upon its own initiative, to identify issues of medical care, research, and education. Dr. Kenneth I. Shine is president of the Institute of Medicine.

The National Research Council was organized by the National Academy of Sciences in 1916 to associate the broad community of science and technology with the Academy's purposes of furthering knowledge and advising the federal government. Functioning in accordance with general policies determined by the Academy, the Council has become the principal operating agency of both the National Academy of Sciences and the National Academy of Engineering in providing services to the government, the public, and the scientific and engineering communities. The Council is administered jointly by both Academies and the Institute of Medicine. Dr. Bruce M. Alberts and Dr. William A. Wulf are chairman and vice chairman, respectively, of the National Research Council.

The project that is the subject of this report is supported by funds provided by the National Institute of Justice, U.S. Department of Justice. Any opinions, findings, conclusions, or recommendations expressed in this publication are those of the author(s) and do not necessarily reflect the view of the organizations or agencies that provided support for this project.

International Standard Book Number 0-309-06192-X
Library of Congress Catalog Card Number 98-87275

Additional copies of this report are available from:

National Academy Press, 2101 Constitution Avenue, N.W., Lockbox 285, Washington, D.C. 20055; (800) 624-6242 or (202) 334-3313 (in the Washington metropolitan area); Internet, http://www.nap.edu

WORKSHOP PARTICIPANTS

ROBERT M. HAUSER (*Workshop Chair*), Institute for Research on Poverty, University of Wisconsin, Madison

CHRISTINE BACHRACH, Center for Population Research, National Institute of Child Health and Human Development, National Institutes of Health

PAULA BAKER, Center for Human Resource Research, Ohio State University

RICHARD BAVIER, Office of Management and Budget

BENNETT BERTENTHAL, National Science Foundation

STEPHEN BUKA, Harvard University

LARRY BUMPASS, University of Wisconsin, Madison

LESLIE CHRISTOVICH, Food and Nutrition Service, U.S. Department of Agriculture

ROBERT DALRYMPLE, Office of Analysis and Evaluation, Food and Nutrition Service, U.S. Department of Agriculture

JOHN ENDAHL, Food and Nutrition Service, U.S. Department of Agriculture

JEFF EVANS, National Institute of Child Health and Human Development, National Institutes of Health

AMY FINKELSTEIN, Council of Economic Advisers

SARAH FRIEDMAN, National Institute of Child Health and Human Development, National Institutes of Health

JOHN GOERING, Office of Research, U.S. Department of Housing and Urban Development

JEANNE GRIFFITH, Division of Science Resources Studies, National Science Foundation

MARIA HANRATTY, Council of Economic Advisers

SUSAN HAUAN, U.S. Department of Health and Human Services

DON HERNANDEZ, Board on Children, Youth, and Families, National Research Council

SANDRA HOFFERTH, Institute of Social Research, University of Michigan

DAVID HUIZINGA, Institute of Behavioral Science, University of Colorado

GUILLERMINA JASSO, New York University

NANCY KIRKENDALL, U.S. Office of Management and Budget

ROBERT KOMINSKI, Population Division, U.S. Bureau of the Census

PAMELA LATTIMORE, National Institute of Justice, U.S. Department of Justice

MARY CLARE LENNON, National Center for Children in Poverty

ROSE LI, National Institute of Child Health and Human Development, National Institutes of Health

MICHAEL LOPEZ, Administration on Children, Youth, and Families

JOHN LOVE, Mathematica Policy Research, Inc.

v

JENNIFER MADANS, Vital and Health Statistics Systems, National Center for Health Statistics
GILLES MONTIGNY, Statistics Canada
KRISTIN MOORE, Child Trends, Inc.
RANDALL OLSEN, Center for Human Resource Research, Ohio State University
JEFFREY OWINGS, School and Family Longitudinal Studies Program, National Center for Education Statistics
HELEN RAIKES, Administration on Children, Youth, and Families
SARAH REBER, Council of Economic Advisers
KERRY RICHTER, Child Trends, Inc.
PATRICIA RUGGLES, Office of the Assistant Secretary for Planning and Evaluation, U.S. Department of Health and Human Services
MARK SHRODER, U.S. Department of Housing and Urban Development
HOWARD SILVER, Consortium of Social Science Associations
LOUISA TARULLO, Administration on Children, Youth, and Families
KATHERINE TOUT, Child Trends, Inc.
JAMES TRUDEAU, National Institute of Justice, U.S. Department of Justice
J. RICHARD UDRY, Carolina Population Center, University of North Carolina
JOHN VEUM, Bureau of Labor Statistics
CHRISTY VISHER, National Institute of Justice, U.S. Department of Justice
DANIEL WEINBERG, U.S. Bureau of the Census
JERRY WEST, National Center for Educational Statistics, U.S. Department of Education
MARVIN WOLFGANG, University of Pennsylvania
MARTY ZASLOW, Child Trends, Inc.

National Research Council Staff

NANCY GEYELIN, *Project Assistant*, Board on Children, Youth, and Families
JEFFREY KOSHEL, *Study Director*, Committee on National Statistics
ANU PEMMARAZU, *Research Assistant*, Committee on National Statistics
DEBORAH PHILLIPS, *Director*, Board on Children, Youth, and Families
TERRI SCANLAN, *Program Specialist*, Committee on National Statistics
MIRON STRAF, *Director*, Committee on National Statistics
BARBARA BOYLE TORREY, *Executive Director*, Commission on Behavioral and Social Sciences and Education
KIRSTEN WEST, *Research Associate*, Committee on National Statistics
ANDREW WHITE, *Deputy Director*, Committee on National Statistics

Acknowledgments

The Committee on National Statistics and the Board on Children, Youth, and Families would like to thank all who participated in the workshop on longitudinal research on children, sharing their expertise, experiences, and concerns through stimulating discussions and for their thoughts and comments that lent to the shaping of this report. We especially thank Robert Hauser of the University of Wisconsin for serving as chair.

We also gratefully acknowledge the contributions of those who worked to organize the workshop and prepare this report. Miron Straf, Deborah Phillips, and Andrew White led and oversaw the undertaking of the workshop, from its development to the preparation of this report. Kirsten West took the major responsibility for organizing the workshop, preparing an initial draft of the workshop summary and responding to reviewers' comments. Terri Scanlan assisted in organizing the workshop and preparing the report for publication. We are grateful to Anne Bridgman, who made valuable revisions on initial drafts; Barbara Bodling, who provided the editing; and to Eugenia Grohman, who oversaw the review process.

With sadness, we acknowledge the untimely death of our friend and colleague, Marvin E. Wolfgang. He was a distinguished criminologist and scholar of longitudinal surveys of delinquency. We are privileged to have had him join us for this workshop.

This report has been reviewed by individuals chosen for their diverse perspectives and technical expertise, in accordance with procedures approved by the NRC's Report Review Committee. The purpose of this independent review is to provide candid and critical comments that will assist the authors and the NRC in making the published report as sound as possible and to ensure that the report meets institutional standards for objectivity, evidence, and responsiveness to the study charge. The content of the review comments and draft manuscript remain confidential to protect the integrity of the deliberative process.

We wish to thank the following individuals for their participation in the review of this report: Larry Bumpass, Center for Demography and Ecology, University of Wisconsin; Julie DaVanzo, RAND, Santa Monica, California; Greg Duncan, Center for Urban Affairs, Northwestern University; Sara McLanahan, Office of Population Research, Princeton University; William O'Hare, Anne E. Casey Foundation, Baltimore, Maryland; Paul R. Rosenbaum, Department of Statistics, The Wharton School, University of Pennsylvania; and Jay Teachman, Department of Human Development, Washington State University. Although the individuals listed above have provided many constructive comments and suggestions, responsibility for the final content of this report rests solely with the authoring committees and the NRC.

Contents

List of Surveys Represented

British National Child Development Study (NCDS)
    Representative: Paula Baker
Canadian National Longitudinal Survey of Children and Youth (NLSCY)
    Representative: Gilles Montigny
Children and Young Adults of the National Longitudinal Surveys of Youth
    Representative: Randall Olsen
Delinquency in a Birth Cohort in the People's Republic of China
    Representative: Marvin Wolfgang
Early Childhood Longitudinal Study, Birth and Kindergarten Cohorts (ECLS)
    Representative: Jerry West
Early Head Start Research and Evaluation Project
    Representative: John M. Love
National Education Longitudinal Study (NELS:1988)
    Representative: Jeffrey Owings
National Longitudinal Study of Adolescent Health (Add Health)
    Representative: J. Richard Udry
National Longitudinal Survey of Youth, 1979 (NLSY79)
    Representative: Randall Olsen
National Longitudinal Survey of Youth, 1997 (NLSY97)
    Representative: John Veum
New Immigrant Survey Pilot Study
    Representative: Guillermina Jasso

National Institute for Child Health and Human Development Study of Early Child Care
    Representative: Sarah Friedman
Panel Study of Income Dynamics (PSID)
    Representative: Sandra Hofferth
Program of Research on the Causes and Correlates of Delinquency: Denver Youth Survey, Pittsburgh Youth Study, Rochester Youth Development Survey
    Representative: David Huizinga
Project on Human Development in Chicago Neighborhoods
    Representative: Stephen Buka
Survey of Program Dynamics for Assessing Welfare Reform (SPD)
    Representative: Don Hernandez
Wisconsin Longitudinal Study (WLS)
    Representative: Robert M. Hauser

Longitudinal Surveys of Children

Longitudinal Surveys of Children

BACKGROUND

For decision makers at all levels of government, the need to understand what influences the lives of children and youth and to assess the outcomes of policies that affect them has grown in recent years, along with rising pressure for accountability and increasing concern about the problems that affect America's children and youth.

This is a period of enormous change in the circumstances of children and youth, partly as a consequence, but also contributing to pervasive changes in family life. Although the share of children and adolescents in the general population is decreasing, the share of minority and immigrant children and youth is increasing. More children are being raised today in nontraditional families. A large fraction, perhaps as many as a quarter at any given time, live in poverty. An increasing share—now a large majority of all preschool children—receive care outside the home. Many children and youth are victims or perpetrators of crime. All of this is occurring in an era of shifting responsibility for the well-being of children and youth and in a world of increasing demands for greater competence in the workplace.

As growing numbers of policy makers turn to the federal statistical system to help guide them in the development of policies and programs for children and youth, longitudinal data on children hold the key to knowledge about the factors that impede or foster healthy development. Given this continuing interest in monitoring and understanding the lives of children and youth, the Committee on National Statistics and the Board on Children, Youth, and Families of the National Research Council and the Institute of Medicine conducted a workshop on September 12 and 13, 1997, on longitudinal studies of children. The workshop was held to (1) examine conceptual and methodological challenges in surveys that collect longitudinal data on children and their families, (2) encourage and foster information sharing, and (3) support collaboration across otherwise independent longitudinal research initiatives on children and youth. Sponsored by the National Institute of Justice, the workshop brought together principal investigators from a number of major longitudinal surveys on children, other experts in the field, and representatives from federal government agencies.

The Committee on National Statistics and the Board on Children, Youth, and Families have a longstanding interest in this issue. A workshop in 1994 on the integration of federal statistics on children and families was motivated by the pressing need for statistics to inform policy makers who formulate, implement, and analyze policies for children, youth, and families. At the conclusion of that workshop, participants stressed the importance of sustaining the debate on improving longitudinal surveys on children. A salient goal is to ensure that relevant data are collected and made available on a timely basis (National Research Council, 1995).

Sixteen surveys were represented at the 1997 workshop. The surveys at the workshop are major longitudinal surveys that either concentrate solely on datasets of children or have a major component that involves data on children. Since the workshop was intended to serve as a forum for informal exchange among the participants, it was deemed appropriate to keep the number of surveys represented fairly small, in order to create a conducive atmosphere for discussion. The workshop participants consisted of the principal investigators of the surveys (or an appropriate representative), invited guests from organizations and federal agencies interested in the issues relevant to the study of children, and representatives from the sponsoring agency. All present were encouraged to contribute their viewpoints and participate in the workshop discussions. A list of participants and the surveys represented appears in the front of this report.

The surveys represented at the workshop were selected on the basis of such factors as scope, design, and stage of completion, in order to obtain numerous perspectives. The surveys cover a wide range of substantive areas of child development and well-being, including health, education, delinquency and crime, child care, and participation in social welfare programs. The surveys represented at the workshop are in various stages of completion. Some have been in the field for many years; others are still in their early stages. A few are not yet in the data collection phase. Most, however, are in some stage of development or reassessment, in the initial planning stage, developing a supplement, or designing a follow-on protocol. The surveys vary in scope and span many age groups and segments of the population, including immigrant children and children in inner-city environments. Some surveys are nationally representative; others include multiple sites; and still others involve intensive data collection in a single site.

Some collect data in personal interviews; others rely on observation, administrative records, or time diaries to supplement the data. In addition to surveys conducted in the United States, longitudinal surveys in England, Canada, and China were represented at the workshop.

To facilitate the workshop discussion, a summary overview for each survey was prepared, providing a brief introduction, a statement about the central substantive issues that guided development of the survey, the study design, the sampling strategies, and the constructs being assessed. Data collection instruments and methods also were listed, as was information on the current status of the survey. This information appears in Appendixes A and B.

The workshop agenda was structured to allow for discussion of cross-cutting methodological and conceptual issues, identification of common policy questions, and consideration of mechanisms for ongoing information sharing. In advance of the workshop, participants prepared brief statements noting special challenges and issues, and time was allotted at the workshop to address these concerns in open discussion. Ample time was allowed for brainstorming and additional open exchange among the participants. The agenda appears in Appendix C.

Although the agenda was designed to be flexible, allowing ample time for discussions and time for participants to raise issues of particular significance to their survey, the workshop did not cover many methodological issues of relevance and importance to longitudinal studies in general and longitudinal studies on children in specific.

This report is intended to be used by representatives from federal and state agencies engaged in research, data collection, program evaluation, and policy analysis pertaining to children and youth; administration officials engaged in policy formulation, implementation, and evaluation; congressional staff; public and private sponsors of research on children, youth, and families; and data users in academic communities and research organizations that focus on children and their well-being.

MAJOR ISSUE AREAS

Four major issue areas emerged from the workshop: (1) theoretical issues, (2) methodological issues, (3) adequacy of data, and (4) dissemination of data. The topics represent the participants' cross-cutting observations and reflect the issues and challenges researchers face. Participants' ideas regarding the next steps to be taken in conducting longitudinal research on children and youth appear at the end of the report.

Since longitudinal studies span many years, often more than a decade, providing data that are representative of the current population becomes a challenge; such data are usually better collected by cross-sectional surveys. Although many longitudinal surveys are designed to provide continuous representation of the population or of sampled cohorts, it can be difficult to continue to meet the changing demands for policy relevance, which is often facilitated by including new question sequences into the study design. In addition to the theoretical and methodological issues is the need for critical assessments of existing data on children, child development, and child well-being and careful consideration of topics to be added to future data collections on children, youth, and their families. At the core of the discussions was the issue of ensuring that data will be available to answer current and future policy questions, many of which concern issues of cause and effect and are increasingly focused on children and youth.

Participants agreed that children and youth constitute a special population for research, involving both constraints and challenges. A range of developmental issues across infancy, childhood, and youth must be addressed and studied. Thus, traditional survey instruments or interviewing techniques often require reassessment when the focus shifts from adults to children as respondents and subjects or to adults as informants about children or adolescents. Perceptions of respondent burden and cooperation may also differ. Special consents often must be granted when children and adolescents are involved as survey subjects.

Theoretical Issues

Workshop participants discussed the extent to which specific theoretical perspectives guided the design of the surveys. They also discussed the theoretical underpinnings of measurements used in longitudinal studies on children, including such specific measures as those used in capturing issues related to child development.

Theoretical Models

Workshop participants debated the extent to which their surveys were guided by a specific theoretical framework or based on a specific theoretical model—for example, a model derived from developmental psychological principles or perspectives founded on behavioral genetics, sociological, or biological theories. The National Institute of Child Health and Human Development's (NICHD) Study of Early Child Care was guided by developmental psychology, and the hypotheses to be tested by the study were spelled out prior to data collection, providing a unique opportunity to study both predicted and unpredicted connections between processes and outcomes. This appears to be an exception rather than the rule. Most study designs are not based on a specific theoretical model. Some participants thought that surveys, especially those conducted by the federal government, could not commit to one specific theoretical model. However, participants agreed that, in order to study children and youth longitudinally and to capture transitions in their development, it is important to know what is expected to happen at different ages. Experts agree that a good survey design offers data to a broad audience and allows for a range of hypotheses to be tested. The measures included in the study usually are not driven by one specific model of development. Once the data have been collected, they can inform questions that arise from a range of theoretical and policy perspectives.

The National Longitudinal Study of Adolescent Health (Add Health) serves as an example of a survey that allows comparisons of sociological and biological models. Based on a behavioral genetics design, it links children with different kinds of genetic relatedness. A large sampling frame allows the study of combinations, such as twins, half-siblings, cousins, and biologically unrelated children living in the same household, as well as the more common nontwin siblings. At the same time, its sample provides aggregations of respondents into peer, family, school, and neighborhood context that are central to prevailing ecological theories of development.

Workshop participants agreed that, in order to understand outcomes for children and youth, surveys must include environmental influences that go beyond the home to the neighborhood, child care provider, school settings, and perhaps even the work site and the judicial system. The workshop participants also agreed that surveys need to consider multiple dimensions of child well-being. Many of the more recent surveys represented at the workshop incorporated this insight into their design. For example, the Early Childhood Longitudinal Study assesses children along a number of physical, social, emotional, and cognitive development dimensions—an important distinction from past educational studies that focused almost exclusively on cognitive outcomes. Thus, this study is guided by a framework of children's development and schooling, emphasizing the child and the interaction among the child's family, school, and community. Analyses of the Early Head Start Evaluation will be based in part on the participating programs and theories of change, which specify their expected outcomes and program strategies for achieving them.

Participants called for research and development of short scales for implementation in surveys. Such research should include considerations of alternative methodological approaches, such as balanced incomplete block spiraling (BIB). In this approach, a many-item scale is split into overlapping blocks, and each person answers only a few items. The participants also considered it important to provide realistic guidelines about what constructs are amenable to being assessed in the context of surveys.

Measurements

Workshop participants discussed the goal of assessing children's development in several critical domains, combined with the practical constraints imposed by a survey's methodology. Critical domains of child development include cognitive and noncognitive areas (e.g., physical, social, and emotional development). Processes as well as outcomes should be captured (e.g., approaches to learning and approaches to problem solving). The child development community and the survey research community offer different perspectives on the best data collection strategies and often use different instrument validation tools. The participants, very aware of these issues, concurred that it is an enormous challenge to get valid data on children and their development in the context of a survey.

Participants recognized that the scales administered in assessments must be appropriate for the ages of the children and youth in the study and that they must be recognized by experts in the field—such as developmental psychologists—as valid and accurate indicators. However, financial and human project resources impose practical constraints on how intensively any given aspect of child development can be assessed. The participants thought, for example, that current clinical assessment scales are not always appropriate for surveys. These scales or batteries are developed for clinical use with individuals—where accuracy is critically important—or for research within relatively small and homogeneous samples. When the objective is not clinical treatment but the estimation and description of relationships among variables and the study population is heterogeneous, it may be both valid and necessary in terms of time and cost of assessment to work with a well-designed subset of assessment items that can be readily administered in the survey setting. Furthermore, the personnel available to administer the assessments often are not professionals in the field but hired data collectors who must be given special training. Thus, the assessment scales must be brief and amenable to standardization and computerized instrumentation.

Workshop participants addressed how information is gained from direct and indirect assessments. Indirect assessments are included in many surveys and may involve videotaping behavior. For example, the Early Head Start evaluations videotape interactions between mothers and children at three ages. Most surveys depend on a mixture of assessment methodologies.

Measurement of change is a central goal in longitudinal studies, and the participants discussed adaptive testing methodologies to achieve good measurement throughout the range of skills being assessed. It is important that floor and ceiling effects be avoided, e.g., that test items allow for detection of growth for children performing at both the lower and upper end of the distribution of difficulty. The Early Childhood Longitudinal Study's kindergarten cohort was offered as an illustration of a survey that uses a two-stage adaptive approach. Here, the degree of success in answering questions early in a test sequence determines the level of difficulty of succeeding questions. This type of approach is also valuable when the time available for testing is limited; children spend most of their testing time responding to items that are at or near their ability level rather than items across the entire ability distribution.

Workshop participants also recognized that language use and capacity influence many assessments. Sometimes, because of a lack of multilingual assessment instruments and multilingual data collectors, assessments are conducted in English even if this is not the subject's first language or the language spoken by the child. Thus, for a study such as the New Immigrant Survey, the design of more appropriate assessment instruments is a critical challenge.

Finally, participants noted the importance of capturing and measuring the impact of children's environments. It is often difficult to separate school effects from neighborhood effects, and the concept of neighborhood is not always clearly conceptualized in the study design. Social science concepts such as cohesion and informal social control may be captured, but measures linking service availability and service utilization at the community level to outcomes for children and youth are lacking. Participants called for better measures of the influence of environment on child development, especially the impact of the neighborhood.

Methodological Issues

Some methodological challenges are inherent to all longitudinal surveys. Providing representative and current data are among such challenges. From its inception, a longitudinal survey collects data into the future from the same observational units. Thus, a survey's design entails using the proper sampling frame to select a sample representative of that frame. Different strategies are used to ensure that the sample remains representative of the universe it purports to represent over time. As the subjects in the sample age, the sample must be refreshed or augmented to compensate for attrition and other changes. The survey must also be designed to ensure that the data provide timely information. Staying current and addressing emerging policy issues continue to be challenges for those who design longitudinal surveys. Some surveys address this need by augmenting the survey scope, adding supplemental modules for occasional coverage of specific topics. These challenges face all longitudinal surveys, not just surveys of children. For longitudinal surveys of children, however, workshop participants believed it to be especially important to learn the best ways to track respondents and minimize nonresponse.

Tracking Respondents

Keeping track of respondents who participate in longitudinal surveys—especially those who move or for whom there is no fixed address—is critical to the success of any such survey. It is not uncommon for children to change households, to move as a household, or to change schools during the year or between years with or without changing home addresses, creating both operational and analytical difficulties. This is a particular challenge for those who want to include special populations, such as children involved in foster care, children whose parents have separated or divorced, and children of high-risk families (e.g., low-income families). Although time-tested procedures for tracking respondents are in place, workshop participants emphasized the importance of keeping up with technological advances, such as World Wide Web or CD-ROM-based address directories, and using innovative approaches to track respondents, including establishing toll-free phone numbers for respondents to contact researchers, offering monetary incentives, and developing special tracking networks.

Minimizing Nonresponse

Nonresponse is an issue for all those involved in carrying out surveys, but it is of particular concern in longitudinal data collections, especially those that gather data from different sources and multiple respondents. Obtaining respondents' cooperation is not a trivial issue, but workshop participants agreed that this is an area where survey designers can exercise some control. Perceptions of the burdens on respondents and their impact on response rates may vary by the socioeconomic status of the families involved as well as the children's ages. Workshop participants concurred that too little is known about what works and for whom, particularly with reference to subsamples of children, youth, and families. They called for more tests of the types of incentives, especially monetary, that successfully reduce nonresponse.

Adequacy of Data

Workshop participants agreed that abundant data on children and youth already have been collected but that there is little or no recent synthesis across subject-matter areas. Suggestions about ways to inventory and synthesize what is known included mining existing datasets to create topic-specific data files, creating collections of topic-specific research papers, and engaging in joint analysis efforts to enhance the knowledge of best current practices in the field. It is evident that data are lacking on some variables of keen current interest. Little is known about how children and adolescents spend their time, for example, or about the role of fathers in children's development. Participants expressed concern about the paucity of relevant policy data to study the effects on children and youth of program and policy changes in such areas as welfare reform. The ensuing discussion focused on three areas in which data appear to be lacking or inadequate: time use, fatherhood, and program evaluation.

Time-Use Data

Time use of children and adolescents has received increased attention in recent years, but there is little current empirical data on the topic. A few of the surveys represented at the workshop collect such data through diaries. For example, in the Panel Study of Income Dynamics (PSID), parents or caregivers record children's activities in diaries for each child for two 24-hour periods, weekends and weekdays, from birth through age 12. When completed, the diaries are collected and the entries are edited by interviewers.

Workshop participants discussed the value of such data to get a picture of how children and youth use their time and to gain insights about input from parents, child care providers, and school personnel. A diary is a unique data collection method and perhaps one of the best ways to get a picture of how children use their time and to gain insight about input from their parents, child care providers, and school personnel. However, the workshop participants expressed a general concern about the validity of time-use data and concurred that more research is needed on measurement errors.

Fatherhood Data

Data on fathering and father-child interactions are inadequate. Workshop participants called specifically for more survey research on the impact of fathers on child development, as relatively little is known about the roles that both biological and social fathers play in children's development. Traditionally, mothers are believed to be the best survey respondents for questions regarding their children. But interviewing fathers in addition to mothers may enhance understanding of family dynamics and the context in which children develop. This approach poses additional methodological challenges and costs, especially when interviewing fathers involves tracking and locating absent ones (Peters et al., 1996).

The impact of absent fathers on children's development is a topic of current national concern, and several of the studies represented at the workshop collect data on this topic. For example, the PSID gathers information from mothers about absent fathers and makes an attempt to locate them, often successfully. Beyond direct assessments of fathering, recent data from the Add Health study concur with previous findings that youth for whom father presence or absence is identified show different behavioral profiles than youth for whom this information is lacking altogether. There appear to be many ways in which fatherhood data can enhance understanding of child development. The NICHD is funding a major interview and videotaping survey of the fathers of Early Head Start children.

Program Evaluation Data

At the workshop, considerable discussion focused on the extent to which existing surveys can contribute to efforts to assess the effects of recent governmental policy changes on children, youth, and families. In particular, participants debated the ways in which survey data can provide information about the impact of recent welfare reform legislation[1] on the outcomes of children and youth. In

---

[1]The Personal Responsibility and Work Opportunity Reconciliation Act of 1996 (Public Law 104-193) made sweeping changes in public assistance for children, youth, and families. Among its major

general, few surveys include both the child outcome data and input data, such as program participation, that are needed to link findings to welfare reform. Moreover, given the extensive state- and county-level variations in implementation of the law, data that can be disaggregated to this level are needed. Few if any of the existing surveys can provide this level of data. The Early Head Start Evaluation includes information from local site visits that might be useful in monitoring the effects of welfare reform. The Census Bureau's Survey of Program Dynamics (SPD) also would provide much-needed data (see Appendix A for additional details on this survey). Novel child and family content is due to be piloted in spring 1999; however, at the time of the workshop the amount of information that will be collected was still being determined. Overall, the experts believe that available surveys can provide only inferential insights into the effects of welfare reform on children and youth and that most are not able to track the effects.[2]

Overall, workshop participants cited as a challenge the need to obtain pre- and post-reform data to determine what outcomes can be attributed to policy change. They also noted the special challenges inherent in program evaluations that differ from those facing national longitudinal studies. These include the collection of program and policy data and the critical importance of considering when it is appropriate to assess program or policy outcomes. Often, the desire to study groups that are representative of a national population is at odds with the desire to study comparable groups receiving competing treatments.

Dissemination of Data

Workshop participants believed public release and dissemination of data to be a controversial and challenging issue. Tensions exist surrounding the wide-

---

reforms, it replaced Aid to Families with Dependent Children with Temporary Assistance to Needy Families, which is a time-limited and not an entitlement program. It eliminated many benefits for legal immigrants who arrived in the United States after August 22, 1996, the date of the law's enactment, and left many other decisions about immigrant eligibility to state discretion.

[2]Other longitudinal surveys being conducted to monitor the effects of welfare reform on children, youth, and families include the JOBS Child Outcomes Study (since 1989, Child Trends, Inc., has conducted a study of the impact of the federal JOBS program on children's health, cognitive development, adjustment, and school outcomes in three sites across the country); the Measuring Child Outcomes Under Various State Welfare Waivers project (with support from the U.S. Department of Health and Human Services, NICHD, and private foundations, Child Trends is working with the states of California, Connecticut, Florida, Iowa, Illinois, Indiana, Michigan, Minnesota, Ohio, Oregon, Vermont, and Virginia to assess the implications for children of state welfare reforms begun under waivers to the old AFDC program and continued under TANF); and the Multi-City Study of the Effects of Welfare Reform on Children and Families (a multidisciplinary study being carried out by Johns Hopkins University, this five-year project is gathering and analyzing longitudinal data in Boston, Chicago, and San Antonio—National Research Council, 1998).

spread interest in timely release of datasets to the public, concerns about proper documentation to guard against inappropriate uses of data, and fears about breaches of respondent confidentiality. Data release and disclosure were cited as among the most common challenges faced by those conducting longitudinal surveys. Although the time between data collection and public release varies, it has become increasingly simple to obtain data with the advent of computer disks, the Internet, and electronic data file transfers.

Universal availability of data, however, raises a concern for proper analytical applications of data (e.g., when and how to use weighting, how to portray outcome measures). Furthermore, the trend is to seek ways to link data across datasets and to increase the knowledge base for smaller geographic units. It is central in this context to ensure that, when data are made available to the public, the process does not inadvertently disclose information about individual respondents. In addition to confidentiality, consent is a crucial issue for those involved in releasing data, such as videotaped data from longitudinal surveys. Amid growing concerns about confidentiality and privacy in this computer era, workshop participants agreed that efforts are needed both to develop protocols for the research community and to educate the public on these matters.

Early Data Release

The public's need for up-to-date information, especially for program evaluations, puts pressure on researchers to release data as quickly as possible after collection. In the past, research findings made their way into print, and the data themselves were eventually released to the public and then archived. Today, data are often available simultaneously with or before extensive analysis takes place. Early releases, however, frequently do not include all data adjustments, such as adjustments for nonresponse or imputations for missing data.

For some data collections, initial data analyses occur inhouse before the data files are made available to the public. For example, there is a two-year inhouse research period before data from the Denver Youth Survey of the Program of Research on the Causes and Correlates of Delinquency are available for public use. In contrast, the National Center for Education Statistics (NCES) believes that its first priority is to produce statistics for the public and to make the data available to the public as quickly as possible, although some restrictions are imposed. In the NICHD Study of Early Child Care, early site-specific data files were released only to the principal investigators at the site that provided the data, not to all sites involved in the study. These data have not yet been released to the public. At times, data files are released under contractual arrangements only. The Add Health study has released data to the public using only half of the sample; the full set of data is available only to contractual users of the data.

Universal Availability of Data

Computer technology makes it possible for a broad audience with various levels of statistical sophistication to access data from surveys. Workshop participants discussed whether users who have not been involved in a survey's design and data collection can fully understand the complexities of the data collected and questioned the ability of less experienced users to apply proper weights to data extracts or to calculate standard errors. Participants agreed that a survey's protocol must be clear, concise, and accessible to the user community and that efforts should be made to facilitate proper use of the data—for example, by providing computer programs for computing standard errors, rather than requiring users to do their own calculations. Beyond such efforts to avoid misuses of data, workshop participants did not think they should take responsibility for the public's use or interpretation of data. On the contrary, they thought that further analyses of data may lead to innovative ways of thinking about patterns in the data, new insights, and discoveries. And although ample opportunity exists for individuals to misinterpret data that are disseminated, peer reviews serve as gatekeepers for the scientific community.

Data Linkages and Confidentiality

In addition to proper analytical applications of data, universal availability also raises concern about confidentiality and data disclosure. The trend in the social sciences field is to seek ways to link data (e.g., linking survey data to state administrative data) and thus to increase the range of information that is available for smaller geographical units. Administrative data can also be used as a validation tool to confirm individual reports of, for example, public benefits received. Data can be linked in many different ways. Some longitudinal studies are designed to pursue personal links to respondents, such as ties to absent fathers, parents, children, and siblings. Some studies also link children and adolescents to their child care providers and their educational environment. Often, a respondent's Social Security number is required for such links to be made successfully, opening the door to perceptions of inappropriate intrusion.

The practice of data linkages raises many ethical issues. It remains a challenge to ensure that data confidentiality is not breached. Workshop participants discussed techniques for disguising the identity of respondents, such as different strategies of adding noise to the data (e.g., random components that increase variability but, on average, do not contribute to the magnitude of estimated effects). Depending on the techniques used, it may be possible to identify an individual respondent using just a few variables. Participants agreed that, although linkages across datasets can enhance the utility of survey data in many ways, caution is warranted, particularly when samples of children and youth are involved for whom issues of custody, juvenile crime, and consent for medical procedures, to name a few, are both highly salient and very sensitive with regard to the protection of confidentiality.

The Statistics Canada survey—Canadian National Longitudinal Survey of Children and Youth—addresses the issue of confidentiality by offering to run programs for its customers. In the United States, it is common practice for a federal agency such as the Census Bureau to swear in a data user as a special employee if microlevel data files rather than aggregated data files are to be analyzed. The Census Bureau has set up two research data centers—one at Carnegie Mellon University and one at the bureau's Boston regional office, and a third center is being created—where researchers work directly with confidential data.

The NCES has a licensing arrangement with organizations that have access to restricted-use data files. These files contain individually identifiable information. NCES will lend restricted-use data only to qualified organizations in the United States using a strict licensing process. Under the terms of the license, NCES has the right to conduct unannounced, unscheduled inspections of the data user's site to assess compliance with the provisions of the license.

Consent

Data disclosure becomes even more controversial when the data collection process entails videotaping interviews or behavior. For example, several studies collect data by observing mother-child interactions. When videotaped, respondents are inherently identifiable. In such situations it is often necessary to obtain several types of consent. One type might be to collect the data; another might be to use the data (e.g., use of the data might be allowed solely for educational purposes). Furthermore, consent alone may not always be enough. Respondents may not be aware of the full implications of consent when the data are public, which may lead to a level of disclosure of the data that was not intended. As stated above, when collecting data on minors, the consent issues of adoption, custody, and juvenile crime may be of concern.

NEXT STEPS

Workshop participants proposed a number of ideas for meeting the challenges facing longitudinal survey research on children, including the following:

1. *Developing a guide for interviewing children and youth.* Workshop participants emphasized the usefulness of developing a guide for conducting research on children and youth in the context of survey research. Such a guide would facilitate interviews and ensure that data collection is based on tested principles and best practices in the field. Though the issue has been addressed in various settings and has appeared in different research papers, participants were

not aware of any systematic attempt to synthesize existing knowledge on how best to collect survey data on children and youth. Participants were unaware of guides or handbooks on this issue, only clinical assessment guides.

2. *Developing short-item assessments.* The current practice for collecting data on child development is to apply existing standardized assessment scales. Such scales are often too long and too difficult to administer in a survey where only a short period of time is available for data collection. Workshop participants called for research to develop short-item assessments and learn which constructs are amenable to short-term assessments and which are not. The tools must then be validated and recognized as standard measurement tools. Furthermore, short forms and adaptive testing strategies need to be developed to be utilized with current standard instruments.

3. *Embedding studies and experimental components into longitudinal surveys.* Workshop participants discussed the value of embedding smaller methodological studies or data collections into longitudinal surveys on children. For example, it may be necessary to embed smaller studies into ongoing national initiatives in order to ensure that the data are relevant and that they address current policy questions. Such efforts may involve embedding observational modules or small-scale experiments. Participants called for research into the best strategies for incorporating smaller methodological research projects into larger studies, citing the Wisconsin Longitudinal Survey as a good example of this strategy. They also stressed the need for funding for such methodological research, suggesting that agencies that fund larger ongoing studies be urged to set aside money for embedding studies and experimental components in them.

4. *Ensuring timely dissemination of data while preserving confidentiality.* While workshop participants agreed that data should be made available to the public on a timely basis, they noted that subjects' confidentiality must always be of utmost concern. Preliminary files could be released as research files with appropriate caveats, they suggested. They further agreed that, because some users may have difficulty understanding how to use data from longitudinal datasets, different strategies for ensuring that data users analyze and interpret data properly should be investigated. Strategies to educate data users on how to properly interpret data include workshops at professional conferences, short courses offered by sponsoring agencies, and intern and visiting scholar (fellowship) programs.

5. *Adding topics to existing and new datasets.* Balancing coverage and content and the need to stay current in data collection is a major challenge to longitudinal studies. At times, researchers might find it necessary to augment the scope of a study already in progress. A central core of topics may be addressed initially and consistently and then new ones might be addressed in supplementary modules over the course of the survey. Issues discussed in this context at the workshop were (1) the role of fathers; (2) the well-being of immigrant children

and children of immigrants; (3) the resource needs of families with children with disabilities; (4) neighborhood and community impacts, including data on service availability and utilization; and (5) the gathering of information needed to consider genetic influences. Adding these and other topics to datasets may involve supplementing the original survey team with, for example, behavioral geneticists, urban planners, and experts in special education to assure a more interdisciplinary approach. New research initiatives may also involve collaborative secondary analytical work focused on specific questions, including those that address the topics listed above.

       6. *Collecting data to measure the effects of program and policy changes.* Workshop participants expressed concern that existing national longitudinal surveys do not collect sufficient data to assess the impacts of program and policy changes, such as changes in welfare programs, food assistance and nutrition programs, or health insurance coverage. They cited the 1996 federal welfare reform legislation as a case in point. They were highly supportive of ongoing efforts to monitor the effects of this legislation on children and youth but expressed concern about the lack of a nationally representative longitudinal survey designed with the assessment of welfare reform on children and youth as one of its goals. Participants thought that a workshop on this topic alone would be fruitful.

REFERENCES

National Research Council and Institute of Medicine
     1995   *Integrating Federal Statistics on Children: Report of a Workshop.* Committee on National Statistics and Board on Children, Youth, and Families, National Research Council and Institute of Medicine. Washington, D.C.: National Academy Press.
     1998   *New Findings on Poverty and Child Health and Nutrition: Summary of a Research Briefing.* Anne Bridgman and Deborah Phillips, eds. Board on Children, Youth, and Families. Washington, D.C.: National Academy Press.
Peters, H. Elizabeth, L. Argys, J. Brooks-Gunn, and J. Smith
     1996   Contributions of Absent Fathers to Child Well-being: The Impact of Child Support Dollars and Father-Child Contact. Paper presented at the Conference on Father Involvement, October 10-11. NICHD Family and Child Well-being Network, Bethesda, Md.

Appendixes

APPENDIX
A

Survey Descriptions

This appendix provides detailed descriptive information for each of the surveys that were represented at the workshop. These summary overviews include a brief introduction, a statement about the central substantive issues that guided development of the survey, the study design, the sampling strategies, and the constructs being assessed. Data collection instruments and methods are also listed, as well as information on the current status of the survey. All of the information appearing in this appendix was reviewed and approved by the survey's principal investigator and was current at the time of publication of this report. An attempt was made to ensure the consistency of the information provided for each survey, but for some surveys certain information was not available. The information on the surveys provided in Appendix A was then summarized and appears in table format in Appendix B.

Dataset Name:	British National Child Development Study (NCDS)
Sponsoring Organization:	National Birthday Trust Fund (London)
Data Collection Organization:	Social Statistics Research Unit, City University, London
Principal Investigators:	John Bynner and Peter Shepherd Social Statistics Research Unit, City University, London

Purpose:

The NCDS is a continuing multidisciplinary longitudinal study that takes as its subjects all those living in Great Britain who were born March 3-9, 1958. It has its origins in the Perinatal Mortality Survey. Sponsored by the National Birthday Trust Fund, the NCDS was designed to examine social and obstetric factors associated with stillbirth and death in early infancy among the 17,000 children born in Great Britain in that one week. It was the second in a series of three such perinatal studies, the others being based on a week's births in 1946 and 1970. Each has formed the basis of a continuing longitudinal study.

Design:

The sample size is approximately 16,500 and includes all persons born in Great Britain the week of March 3-9, 1958. In 1991 a random sample of children of one-third of the NCDS respondents (age 33) was added. No subpopulations were oversampled.

Periodicity:

To date, there have been five attempts to trace all members of the birth cohort in order to monitor their physical, educational, and social development. These were carried out by the National Children's Bureau in 1963 (NCDS1), 1969 (NCDS2), 1974 (NCDS3), and 1981 (NCDS4) and by the Social Statistics Research Unit, City University, in 1991 (NCDS5).

In addition, in 1978, contact was made with the schools attended by members of the birth cohort at the time of the second follow-up in 1974 in order to obtain details of public examination entry and performance. Similar details were sought from sixth-form colleges and other education colleges, and so forth, where these were identified by schools.

Content:

The major topics covered by the survey include factors associated with birth outcomes, family formation, employment, education, training, housing, income, health, smoking, drinking, and voluntary activities. Also included are children's cognitive, socioemotional, and behavioral outcomes.

Contexts studied include the family, school, and community. With regard to the type of data collection, interviews are conducted with parents, teachers, spouses, cohabitees, and children. Medical exams and educational tests also are used as data collection instruments. Planned linkage capacities include census data and school records.

Contact:

John Bynner
Peter Shepherd
NCDS User Support
Social Statistics Research Unit
City University
Northhampton Square
London ECIV 0HB
Phone: (0171) 477-8484
Fax: (0171) 477-8583
E-mail: ncds@ssru.city.ac.uk

Robert Michael
University of Chicago
Harris Graduate School
   of Public Policy
1155 E. 60th St.
Chicago, Illinois 60637
Phone: (312) 702-9623
Fax: (312) 702-0926

Dataset Name:	Canadian National Longitudinal Survey of Children and Youth (NLSCY)
Sponsoring Organizations:	Human Resources Development Canada Statistics Canada
Data Collection Organization:	Special Surveys Division, Statistics Canada
Principal Investigators:	Gilles Montigny, Project Manager Special Surveys Division, Statistics Canada Susan McKellar, Project Coordinator Human Resources Development Canada

Purpose:

The purpose of the NLSCY is to collect information over time on critical factors affecting the development of children in Canada. The NLSCY is the first nationwide household survey on child health, development, and well-being in Canada. Data on the prevalence of and interaction among various characteristics and conditions will assist policy makers in understanding the processes that modify risk and protect and encourage the healthy development of children. Such information will enhance the capacity of various partners in society to develop effective strategies, policies, and programs to help children succeed in our changing society.

Description:

The NLSCY follows a sample of children (22,831) ages 0 to 11 in 1994-1995 from infancy to adulthood, collecting information every two years. Children are the statistical unit. For the first three data collections, information is collected from a person knowledgeable about the child (in most cases the child's mother). Children 10 and over are asked to complete a questionnaire; teachers and school principals are asked to provide information on school-aged children and their schools also by completing a questionnaire. The survey casts a wide net, gathering information on children, families, schools, and communities.

Objectives:

The primary objective of the NLSCY is to develop a national database on the characteristics and life experiences of Canadian children as they grow from infancy to adulthood. The more specific objectives are (1) to determine the prevalence of various characteristics and risk factors of children and youth in Canada and (2) to monitor the impact of such risk factors, life events, and protective factors on the development of these children. Underlying these objectives is the need to (1) fill an existing information gap regarding the characteristics and experiences of Canadian children, particularly in their early years; (2) focus on all aspects of the child in a holistic manner (i.e., child, family, school, and community); and (3) explore subject areas that are amenable to policy intervention and that affect a significant segment of the population.

Study Design:

The first NLSCY collection took place in 1994-1995. Some 13,439 households (22,831 children) participated. In addition, information on some 2,300 children was collected in the territories. The sample was divided into seven age groups: children 0-11 months old, 1 year olds, 2-3 year olds, 4-5 year olds, 6-7 year olds, 8-9 year olds, and 10-11 year olds. The sample included all children ages newborn to 11 years residing in the selected households who were members of the same economic family and who lived the majority of time in the household. A maximum of four children in the age range of measurement were surveyed in each economic family: in families with more than four children under 12, four children were selected randomly. The 1994-1995 children sample is the longitudinal sample and will be followed biennially until adulthood.

In the second cycle the NLSCY sample was upgraded in age groups no longer covered by the longitudinal sample, to maintain coverage of the lower age ranges for cross-sectional purposes. It is anticipated that a similar sample upgrading will take place for the third cycle.

Face-to-face interviews were conducted in children's homes with a person knowledgeable about each child. Children age 10 and over were asked to complete a questionnaire during the interview with the knowledgeable person. Children 4 and 5 years of age (4-6 in cycle 2) were administered a vocabulary test (Peabody Picture Vocabulary Test) during the home interview. For school-age children a follow-up in the school was done by mailing a questionnaire to be completed by the teacher and the school principal. Math and reading comprehension tests were also part of the school follow-up for children in grade 2 and above.

Questionnaire Topics:

• *Household-level information*: Demographic and detailed relationship and dwelling characteristics.
• *Parent questionnaire*: Health, education, labor force activity and income, family functioning, depression, social support, neighborhood.
• *General child questionnaire*: Child care, family and custody history, parenting style, health status and injuries.
• *Child questionnaire (children 0-3)*: Perinatal information, temperament, activities, motor and social development.
• *Child questionnaire (children 4-11)*: education/school experience, lit-

eracy activities, activities and responsibilities, behavior, relationships with others.

• *Children 10 and over (self-completed)*: friends and family, feelings and behavior, school experience, puberty, smoking, alcohol, drugs, self-esteem, activities, health.

• *Teacher questionnaire*: Academic progress and problems of the child, parental involvement, characteristics of the classroom, teaching practices, feeling of efficacy, and teacher characteristics.

• *Principal questionnaire*: Composition of student population, school discipline, attendance and stability of school population, material and human resources, parental involvement.

• *Tests:* Peabody Picture Vocabulary Test, math computation, reading comprehension.

Plans for Future Cycles:

Cycle 3 data collection will be conducted in 1998-1999. With the exception of a new questionnaire for 14 to15 year olds, the rest of the collection instruments should remain relatively stable. In addition, approval from respondents to link to taxation records to derive income variables will be sought. For cycle 4 the plans are to reexamine the current design and collection methodology to adjust to a young adult population. Consideration will be given to introduction of a cohort of newborns, with greater emphasis on a more extensive measure of school readiness.

Available Results and Data Files:

The results of the first cycle of the NLSCY are available, with the exception of the section on family and child custody history and data for the territories. A public microdata file is available and can be purchased from Statistics Canada at a cost of $2,000 (CAN). The public microdata contain weighted and edited estimates. Also available is a collection of articles based on the results of the NLSCY first cycle, grouped in a publication entitled *Growing Up in Canada* (catalog no. 89-550-MPE). The publication can also be purchased from Statistics Canada at a cost of $25 (CAN). Release of the results from the second collection is planned for the fall 1998. A file containing longitudinal and cross-sectional estimates will then be made available.

Contact:

Gilles Montigny
Special Surveys Division
Statistics Canada
Phone: (613) 951-9731
Fax: (613) 951-7333
E-mail: montgil@statcan.ca

Susan McKellar
Applied Research Branch
Human Resources Development Canada
Phone: (819) 953-4230
Fax: (819) 994-2480
E-mail: susan.mckellar@spg.org

Dataset Name:	Children and Young Adults of the National Longitudinal Surveys of Youth
Sponsoring Organizations:	Bureau of Labor Statistics National Institute of Child Health and Human Development
Data Collection Organization:	National Opinion Research Center
Principal Investigator:	Randall Olsen Center for Human Resource Research Ohio State University.

Purpose:

The purpose of this ongoing study is to collect child development information on children born to NLSY79 female respondents and to create a large nationally representative data resource for the study of child outcomes. The data available about the children and their mothers and families create an opportunity to study the effects of parental characteristics and experiences on the well-being and development of children. Following these children into late adolescence and early adulthood offers the chance to examine the effects of development on (1) success in school, (2) transition to work, and (3) family formation.

Content:

The NLSY79 child dataset contains information on health, school and family background, attitudes, cognitive and socioemotional development, and quality of the home environment of the sample children. Reports are also recorded on schooling, grade repetition, school behavior and expectations, peer relations, and religious attendance and training for children 10 and older. Information for these preadolescents is also available on family decision making, school attitudes, work activities, peer relationships, religious attendance, smoking, alcohol and drug use, sexual activity, computer use, and gender roles. The following cognitive, socioemotional, and physiological assessments were administered to age-eligible children during the 1986, 1988, 1990, 1992, and 1996 surveys: Home Observation for Measurement of the Environment (HOME) Abbreviated Scale; Body Parts Scale; Peabody Picture Vocabulary Test (PPVT); Memory for Locations; McCarthy Scale of Children's Abilities; Verbal Memory Subscale; Wechsler Intelligence Scale for Children-Revised; Digit Span Subscale; Peabody Individual Achievement Test (PIAT); Math, Reading Recognition, & Reading Comprehension Subscale; Temperament Scale; Behavior Problems Index; Self-Perception Profile; and Motor & Social Development Scale.

The young adult file for children 15 and older contains details about their employment, education, training, family-related experiences, behaviors, and attributes. Transcript information for schools attended in 1993-1994 or 1994-1995 will be added to the files for release with the 1996 data.

Design:

As of 1994, the NLSY79 Children and Young Adults sample consists of the more than 10,000 children ever born to NLSY79 female respondents. The NLSY79 children may be considered representative of (1) children born to a nationally representative cross-section of women age 29-36 in 1994 and (2) all children born to a nationally representative sample of women age 14-21 in 1979. Of these children, a high percentage of those eligible were assessed in each survey year. Starting in 1994, children 15 or older on the date of interview in the household within the previous two rounds were interviewed regardless of current residence status:

- In 1986, there were 5,255 children; 4,971 were assessed.
- In 1988, there were 6,543 children; 6,266 were assessed.
- In 1990, there were 6,427 children; 5,803 were assessed.
- In 1992, there were 7,255 children; 6,509 were assessed.
- In 1994, there were 6,622 children, not young adults; 6,109 were assessed.
- In 1994, there were 1,240 young adult children; 980 were interviewed.

The NLSY79 child and young adult surveys are an extension of the NLSY79, a comprehensive multipurpose survey of more than 12,600 individuals who have been interviewed annually since 1979. The NLSY79 includes an overrepresentation of black, Hispanic, and (through 1990) economically disadvantaged white respondents. The child interviews, home observations, and assessments are primarily administered in person, with follow-ups every two years. The children range in age from newborns to those in their early 20s. The advisory committee consists of experts in child development, demography, economics, and education.

Plans for Future Waves:

The 1996 child and young adult data were released in 1997. Plans are currently under way for a 1998 child and young adult survey round.

Data and Documentation:

The NLSY79 child and young adult files are available at low cost on compact disk. Child-specific data include information on each child's demographic and family background; pre- and postnatal health history; home environment; child care experience; and all items and scores from the 1986, 1988, 1990, 1992, and 1994 child assessments. Constructed mother-specific variables on the child file include information on each mother's household composition, income and earnings, and education. Software on the CD allows merges between the child and young adult cases and any item from the entire longitudinal main youth record of NLSY79 mothers. Comprehensive documentation and bibliographies are available at no charge. Contact the NLS Public Users Office at the address below or at usersvc@pewter.chrr.ohio-state.edu.

Contact:

Randall Olsen
Center for Human Research
921 Chatham Lane, Suite 200
Columbus, OH 43221
Phone: (614) 442-7300
Fax: (614) 442-7329

Frank Mott
Center for Human Research
921 Chatham Lane, Suite 200
Columbus, OH 43221
Phone: (614) 442-7328
E-mail: mott@pewter.chrr.ohio-state.edu

Dataset Name:	Delinquency in a Birth Cohort in the People's Republic of China
Data Collection Organization:	China Juvenile Delinquency Research Society
Principal Investigator:	Marvin Wolfgang[1]
Investigator's Institution:	University of Pennsylvania

Purpose:

The Delinquency in a Birth Cohort in the People's Republic of China study is a replication of the studies of delinquency in two birth cohorts born in Philadelphia in 1945 and 1958. The China cohort was born in 1973 in Wuhan, a city then with 2 million inhabitants and 29,976 births.

Design:

The size of the birth cohort is equivalent to the Philadelphia cohort studies. Thus far, the study has followed a cohort from the area of Wuhan called Wuchang. Wuchang, which has 500,000 inhabitants, has been the focus of most of the data collection. The study follows a cohort of 5,341 people born in 1973 (2,716 males and 2,625 females). Of this cohort, so far 81 (76 males and 5 females) have a record of delinquency. In the study the characteristics of this group are compared with a control group of 81 nondelinquents from the same birth cohort. The pilot study took place in a section of Wuchang called Yangdo. There were 42,000 inhabitants in 1973 and 366 births (195 males and 171 females). Only 5 (4 males and 1 female) had a delinquency record by the time they were 18 years old.

Self-reports will be attempted in the future.

Periodicity:

The study is expected to continue through the year 2000 and will extend to the entire city of Wuhan, which now has a population of more than 3.4 million. Plans are also to expand the study to other regions of the country and include a self-report delinquency study.

Content, Policy, and Research Issues

Data from the two areas—Wuchang and Yangdo—are collected by 50 re-

---

[1]Dr. Wolfgang passed away in April 1998. Information on this survey can be obtained from the Department of Criminology of the University of Pennsylvania.

search assistants in interviews with subjects, parents, teachers, and neighborhood committees and through examination of police records and census data.

In addition to type of delinquency and data of occurrence, data are obtained on education, type of community, occupation, income, marital status, age, race, sex, family cohesiveness, disciplinary punishments in school, learning attitude, goals in life, and bad habits.

Contact:

University of Pennsylvania
Department of Criminology
3937 Chestnut St.
Philadelphia, PA 19104-3110

Dataset Name:	Early Childhood Longitudinal Study Birth Cohort 2000
Sponsoring Organization:	National Center for Education Statistics U.S. Department of Education
Data Collection Organization:	Westat, Inc.
Principal Investigator:	Jerry West National Center for Education Statistics U.S. Department of Education

Purpose:

To inform decision makers, educational practitioners, researchers, and parents about the ways in which children are prepared for school and how schools and early childhood programs affect the lives of the children who attend them. The birth cohort study is being designed to study children's early learning and development from birth through first grade. It will provide national data on (1) children's status at birth and at various points thereafter; (2) children's transitions to nonparental child care, early education programs, and school; and (3) children's progress during the first two years of elementary school, kindergarten and first grade.

Design:

A nationally representative sample of approximately 15,000 children born during calendar year 2000. The sample will consist of children from different racial, ethnic, and socioeconomic backgrounds. Children will be sampled from birth certificates.

Periodicity:

Children will be selected at birth and followed through the end of first grade. The first data collection will occur within the first six months of birth. Three follow-up data collections are scheduled at 12, 18, and 24 or 30 months of age. Thereafter plans call for annual follow-up data collections.

Content, Policy, and Research Issues:

The design is based on the assumption that children's preparation for school begins at (or before) birth and continues until they enter school for the first time. It is guided by a framework of children's development, care, and schooling that emphasizes the interaction between the child, family, care and education programs, and the community. The importance and interrelatedness of factors that represent the child's health status and social, emotional, and intellectual development are recognized. Parents will be the primary respondents. Data will also be gathered from child care and early education providers, schools and teachers, and the children themselves.

Contact:

Jerry West
National Center for Education Statistics
U.S. Department of Education
555 New Jersey Ave., NW, Room 417B
Washington, DC 20208-5651
Phone: (202) 219-1574
Fax: (202) 219-1728
E-mail: jerry_west@ed.gov

Dataset Name:	Early Childhood Longitudinal Study Kindergarten Class of 1998-99
Sponsoring Organization:	National Center for Education Statistics U.S. Department of Education
Cosponsors:	Head Start Bureau, Office of Special Education U.S. Department of Education Food and Nutrition Services U.S. Department of Agriculture
Data Collection Organization:	Westat, Inc.
Principal Investigator:	Jerry West National Center for Education Statistics U.S. Department of Education

Purpose:

To provide national data on (1) children's status at entry into school; (2) children's transition into school; and (3) children's progression through grade 5 and to study how a wide range of family, school, community, and individual variables affect success in school.

Design:

A nationally representative sample of approximately 23,000 children enrolled in about 1,000 kindergarten programs during the 1998-1999 school year will be selected for study. Both private and public kindergartens offering full- and part-day programs will be selected. The plan is to oversample Asian and Pacific Islander children.

Periodicity:

Surveys will be conducted when child begins kindergarten in the fall and leaves kindergarten in the spring. Follow-up interviews will be conducted in the spring first, third, and fifth grades. A fall first-grade follow-up is planned for 25 percent of the base-year sample (approximately 5,000 children).

Content, Policy and Research Issues:

This study will measure aspects of children's development (physical, social, cognitive, and emotional growth) and their environments (home, school, and classroom) as they enter school for the first time and will examine how these influence children's academic achievement and school experience through grade 5. Data will be collected from the children, their parents/guardians, teachers, and schools.

Contact:

Jerry West
National Center for Education Statistics
U.S. Department of Education
555 New Jersey Ave., NW, Room 417B
Washington, DC 20208-5651
Phone: (202) 219-1574
Fax: (202) 219-1728
e-mail: jerry_west@ed.gov

Dataset Name:	Early Head Start Research and Evaluation Project (EHSREP)

Sponsoring Organization:	Administration on Children, Youth, and Families (ACYF) U.S. Department of Health and Human Services
Data Collection Organizations:	National evaluation contractor: Mathematica Policy Research, Inc., and Columbia University Local research: 15 universities (see attached list)
Principal Investigators:	National evaluation: John M. Love, Project Director Ellen Eliason Kisker and Jeanne Brooks-Gunn, Principal Investigators Helen H. Raikes, Project Monitor Louisa Tarullo, Project Officer Local research: See attached list Esther Kresh, Project Officer

Purpose:

Increasing awareness of the problems facing low-income families with infants and toddlers led ACYF to launch this project in 1995. The Early Head Start Research and Evaluation Project (EHSREP), an intense study of the new Early Head Start (EHS) program, is a far-reaching longitudinal study of infants and toddlers in low-income families. EHS programs account for an increasing percentage of the total Head Start budget, as the needs of pregnant women and families with children up to age 3 become more central to Head Start's mission. EHS now serves families in 175 communities with diverse approaches for enhancing children's and families' development, developing staff, and improving communities. More programs will be added in 1998.

Description:

In September 1995, ACYF awarded a national evaluation contract to Mathematica Policy Research, Inc., and Columbia University, and six months later funded 15 local research investigators. The first wave of 68 programs was funded in September 1995, with 75 more funded a year later. EHS is a comprehensive two-generation program of intensive services that begin before a child is born and concentrate on enhancing the child's development and on supporting families through the critical first three years of the child's life. EHS programs focus activities toward diverse goals within four common cornerstones: child development, family development, staff development, and community building. The EHS Research and Evaluation Project, coordinated by the EHS research consortium of national and local researchers and ACYF, encompasses five major components:

• *An implementation study* to examine service needs and use for low-income families with infants and toddlers, assess program implementation, illuminate pathways to achieving quality, examine program contributions to community change, and identify and explore variations across sites.

• *An impact evaluation* to analyze the effects of EHS programs on children, parents, and families in depth, using an experimental design descriptive study to assess outcomes for program staff and communities.

• *Local research studies* by local researchers to learn more about the pathways to desired outcomes for infants and toddlers, parents and families, staff, and communities.

• *Policy studies* to respond to information needs in areas of emerging policy-relevant issues, including welfare reform, fathers, child care, and children with disabilities.

• *Formats for continuous program improvement* to guide all EHS programs in formative evaluation.

Study Objectives:

• To conduct a rigorous cross-site national impact study.

• To encourage a new generation of research that includes quantitative and qualitative research for understanding the role of program variations (different program approaches and services) and contextual variations (diverse communities, welfare reform, richness of community resources, etc.).

• To create the foundation for a series of longitudinal research studies.

Study Design:

• Approximately 3,000 children (and their families) in 17 sites are randomly assigned to the EHS program or a comparison group.

• At intake, the sample comprises pregnant women and families with children under 12 months of age.

• In other respects, all sample families meet Head Start eligibility guidelines, including having approximately 10 percent infants and toddlers with disabilities.

- Baseline data are collected prior to random assignment.
- Age-based assessments are conducted when children are 14, 24, and 36 months old.
- Intake-based Parent Services Interviews (PSIs) are conducted 6, 15, 24, and 36 months after random assignment.
- Three rounds of site visits are conducted to study program implementation and quality.
- Substudies on welfare reform and fathers are coordinated by EHS consortium work groups.

Questionnaire Topics[2]

- Children's cognitive, language, and social development; health; resiliency; emotional regulation; and parental attachment.
- Child care access, use, and quality of nonfamilial care arrangements (observation and interview).
- Family development, including parent-child relationships, home environment, family functioning, family health, parental involvement, parent self-sufficiency, father involvement.
- Parents' use of program and community services (prenatal care, health, employment, etc.).
- Staff development, including professional development, relationships with parents and children, and morale.
- Community development, including child care quality, collaboration among agencies, services integration, role of welfare reform, and changes in child care systems.

Plans for Future Waves:

Later longitudinal follow-up is possible.

Available Results and Data Files:

A complete dataset will be available following the completion of Mathematica's current contract (in 2000). The following reports will be prepared during the contract:

- *Descriptive Implementation Report*, 1998: Descriptive information about the 17 research programs from site visits and application and enrollment data,

---

[2]Note: Data collection is multi-method, including, in addition to questionnaires, in-person interviews, direct assessments, focus groups, observations, videotaped interactions, and program records.

documentation of key program variations, and presentation of the programs' theories of change.

• *Interim Implementation and Quality Report*, 1998: Snapshot of program quality at the time of the fall 1997 site visits and assessment of service use and service quality based on early PSI data for program families; description of the methodology for assessing full implementation and quality.

• *Final Pathways to Quality Report*, 1999: Analysis of the development of program quality over time and different pathways programs follow to achieve high quality in providing child development services.

• *Interim Report on Service Use*, 1999: Interim report on early service use by program and comparison families.

• *Policy Report*, 1999: Special analyses of EHS data to address important policy topics (to be determined, but could include issues related to welfare reform, child care, etc.).

• *Final Impact Report*, 2000: Full technical report on EHS impacts.

• *Synthesis Report*, 2000: Synthesis of all aspects of the EHS evaluation for a broad audience.

Agencies/Organizations Involved in Planning the Early Head Start Research and Evaluation Project:

Administration on Children, Youth, and Families, Administration for Children and Families, Office of the Assistant Secretary for Planning and Evaluation, National Institute of Child Health and Human Development, Bureau of Maternal and Child Health, Department of Education, Health Resources and Services Administration, and the Department of Health and Human Services Advisory Committee on Services for Families with Infants and Toddlers.

Contact:

John M. Love, Project Director
Mathematica Policy Research, Inc.

P.O. Box 2393
Princeton, NJ 08543-2393
Phone: (609) 275-2245
Fax: (609)-799-0005
E-mail:
jlove@mathematica-mpr.com

Helen H. Raikes, Project Monitor
Administration on Children, Youth, and Families
330 C St., SW, Room 2411
Washington, DC 20011
Phone: (202) 205-2247
Fax: (202) 205-8221
E-mail:
heraikes@acf.dhhs.gov

Early Head Start Local Research Investigators:

University of Arkansas, Little Rock
    Mark Swanson, Robert Bradley, and Richard Clubb
University of California, Los Angeles
    Carollee Howes, Shira Rosenblatt, and Jane Wellencamp
University of Colorado Health Sciences Center
    Robert Emde, JoAnn Robinson, Paul Spicer, Jon Korfmacher, and Norman
    Watt (University of Denver)
Catholic University of America
    Shavaun Wall, Christine Sabatino, Harriet Liebow, and Nancy Taylor
Iowa State University
    Carla Peterson and Susan McBride
University of Kansas
    Judith Carta, Jean Ann Summers, and Jane Atwater
Michigan State University
    Rachel Schiffman, Cynthia Gibbons, Tom Reischl, and Hiram Fitzgerald
University of Missouri, Columbia
    Kathy Thornburg, Mark Fine, and Jean Ispa
New York University
    Mark Spellmann and Catherine Tamis-LaMonde
University of Pittsburgh
    Carol McAllister, Robert McCall, and Beth Green (Portland State
    University)
Medical University of South Carolina
    Susan Pickrel, Michael Brondino, and Richard Faldowski
Utah State University
    Lori Roggman
Harvard University
    Catherine Snow, Barbara Pan, and Catherine Ayoub
University of Washington, School of Nursing
    Kathryn Barnard and Susan Spieker
University of Washington, College of Education
    Joseph Stowitschek and Eduardo Armijo

Dataset Name:	National Education Longitudinal Study of 1988 (NELS:88)

Sponsoring Organization:	National Center for Education Statistics U.S. Department of Education
Data Collection Organization:	National Opinion Research Center
Principal Investigators:	Aurora D'Amico and Jeffrey Owings National Center for Education Statistics U.S. Department of Education

Purpose:

The National Education Longitudinal Study of 1988 (NELS:88) is the most recent in a series of longitudinal studies conducted by the National Center for Education Statistics of the U.S. Department of Education. NELS:88 is designed to assess trends in secondary school education, focusing on the transition into and progress through high school, the transition into postsecondary school and the world of work, and family formation experiences. Data from this study can be used to examine educational issues such as tracking, cognitive growth, and dropping out of school.

Design:

NELS:88 is a longitudinal study of a national probability sample of eighth graders. The base-year student population excluded students with severe mental disabilities, students whose command of the English language was insufficient to understand survey materials, and students with physical or emotional problems that would limit their participation.

The survey used a two-stage stratified clustered sample design. The first stage, selection of schools, was accomplished by a complex design involving two sister pools of schools. The second stage included selection of about 24 to 26 students per school. At the second stage, 93 percent of 26,435 selected students agreed to participate. Hispanic and Asian students were oversampled.

Data were collected via questionnaires from 24,599 students in 1,057 public and private schools from all 50 states and the District of Columbia in the base year. Eighth graders participated in group sessions at their schools, where they completed student questionnaires and cognitive tests. School administrator data were collected from the senior school administrator (usually the principal or headmaster). For base-year teacher data, each school was randomly assigned two of four subject areas of interest (English, math, science, social studies), and teachers were chosen who could provide data for each student respondent in these two subjects. Parent data were obtained through the mail.

For the first (1990) follow-up, all students were surveyed in schools containing 10 or more eligible NELS:88 respondents. Only a subsample of students was surveyed in schools with fewer than 10 students. Because 90 percent of students changed schools between the eighth and tenth grades, it was necessary to subsample schools in this way. The 1990 sample size was more than 19,000 students, and the 1992 sample size was about the same.

The sample was freshened in 1990 and 1992 to give 1990 tenth graders and 1992 twelfth graders who were not in the eighth grade in 1988 some chance of selection into the NELS:88 follow-up. Such students included primarily those who had skipped or repeated a grade between 1988 and the follow-up year and those who had moved to the United States after 1988. This freshening was conducted so that the first and second follow-up samples were representative of U.S. tenth graders in 1990 and U.S. twelfth graders in 1992.

Periodicity:

Base-year data were collected in 1988 and included questionnaires from students, school administrators, and parents; teacher ratings of students; and students' achievement test scores.

The first follow-up of NELS:88 was conducted in 1990. At that time, data were collected by way of a student questionnaire (including a brief new-student questionnaire for new students who were brought into the sample to preserve representativeness), a dropout questionnaire (of base-year respondents who had since left school), a student achievement test, a teacher questionnaire, and a school administrator questionnaire.

A second follow-up was conducted in 1992. Data came from student (original and new) questionnaires, dropout questionnaires, student achievement test scores, school administrator and teacher questionnaires, and a parent questionnaire focusing on the financing of postsecondary education. In the second follow-up, only math and science teachers for each student were surveyed. Academic transcripts were collected for each student. The third follow-up was conducted in 1994, when the students were approximately two years out of high school. Education, work, and family formation characteristics were included in this wave of the survey. The fourth and final follow-up was conducted in 1997.

Content, Policy, and Research Issues

School administrator questionnaire: School, student, and teaching staff characteristics; school policies and practices (e.g., admissions, discipline, grading and testing structure); school governance and climate; and school problems.

Teacher questionnaire: Impressions of the student, the student's school behavior and academic performance, curriculum and classroom instructional practices, school climate and policies, and teacher background and activities. The teacher questionnaire for the second follow-up was only given to math and science teachers, who were asked to rate their own professional qualifications and preparation.

Student questionnaire: Family background and characteristics (including household composition, ethnicity, parental education, economic status), relationship with parents, unsupervised time at home, language use, opinions about self, attitudes, values, educational and career plans, jobs and chores, school life (including problems in school, discipline, peer relations, school climate), school work (homework, course enrollment, attitudes toward school, grade repetition, absenteeism), and extracurricular activities. First follow-up included similar content, as well as information about significant life events, family decision making, and substance abuse. The second follow-up contained similar material, as well as plans for the future, money and work, and an early graduate supplement that contained items about reasons for graduating early and current employment and enrollment. The third follow-up includes information on education, work, and family experiences.

Dropout questionnaire: Reasons for leaving school, school attitudes and experiences, current activities (employment and education), family background, future plans, self-opinion and attitudes, substance abuse, money and work, family composition and events, and language use.

Parent questionnaire: Marital status, household composition, employment, ethnicity, religion, child's school experiences and attendance, child's family life (activities, rules, and regulations) and friends, opinion about and contact with child's school, child's disabilities, educational expectations for child, financial information, and educational expenditures. The second follow-up questionnaire included additional brief questions about neighborhood quality and some supplemental questions for parents new to NELS:88.

Student achievement tests: Reading, math, science, and history/citizenship tests were administered in all waves.

New-student supplement: Provides brief information about language, ethnicity, objects in the home, parents' employment, and grade repetition.

School effectiveness study (SES): This was added to the first follow-up to provide a probability sample of tenth-grade schools, with a sizable and representative within-school sample of students, through which longitudinal school-level analyses could be conducted. Two hundred forty-eight schools participated in the first follow-up SES, and the second follow-up SES returned to 247 of those schools.

Transcript files and course offerings: In the second follow-up, complete high school records were collected for (1) students attending sampled schools in the spring of 1992; (2) all dropouts, dropouts in alternative programs, and early graduates, regardless of school affiliations; and (3) triple ineligibles enrolled in the twelfth grade in the spring of 1991, regardless of affiliation. Triple ineligibles are 1988 eighth graders who were ineligible for the base-year, first follow-up, and second follow-up surveys because of a mental or physical disability or language barrier. The course offering component provides curriculum data from second follow-up school effectiveness study schools.

Because questionnaires were not identical at each wave, all of the information described above and indicated in the checklist is not available for every wave.

The longitudinal design of this study permits examination of changes in young people's lives and the role of schools in promoting growth and positive life outcomes. For example, NELS:88 data can be used to investigate the transition from middle to secondary school, students' academic growth over time, features of effective schools, the process of dropping out of school as it occurs from eighth grade on, the role of the school in helping disadvantaged students, the school experiences and academic performance of language-minority students, and factors associated with attracting students to the study of mathematics and science.

Contact:

Aurora D'Amico
National Center for Education Statistics
555 New Jersey Ave., NW
Washington, DC 20208
Phone: (202) 219-1365
E-mail: Aurora_D'Amico@ed.gov

Dataset Name:	National Longitudinal Study of Adolescent Health (Add Health)

Sponsoring Institution:	National Institute of Child Health and Human Development
Data Collection Organization:	Carolina Population Center University of North Carolina at Chapel Hill
Principal Investigator:	J. Richard Udry Carolina Population Center University of North Carolina at Chapel Hill

Purpose:

Add Health was designed to assess the health status of adolescents and to explore the causes of their health-related behaviors, focusing on the effects of the multiple contexts or environments (both social and physical) in which they live. As a group, adolescents are healthy people. They have survived the vulnerable years of childhood and are decades away from the degenerative diseases of old age. Threats to their health stem primarily from their behavior. Add Health focuses on forces that influence adolescents' behavior, in particular forces residing in the various contexts of their lives: families, friendships, romantic relationships, peer groups, schools, neighborhoods, and communities.

Description:

Add Health was undertaken in response to a mandate by the U.S. Congress in the National Institutes of Health (NIH) Revitalization Act of 1993 (Public Law 103-43, Title X, Subtitle D, Section 1031), which stated that:

> ... the Director of the [National Institute of Child Health and Human Development] shall commence a study for the purpose of providing information on the general health and well-being of adolescents in the United States, including, with respect to such adolescents, information on: (1) the behaviors that promote health and the behaviors that are detrimental to health; and (2) the influence on health of factors particular to the communities in which adolescents reside.

Objectives:

• To assess the mental, physical, and emotional health of adolescents in the United States.
• To explore the causes of their health-related and health-affecting behaviors.

- To examine the contexts in which adolescents reside and how these contexts influence their health.
- To assess the impact of differential individual attributes on health-related behaviors.
- To examine the impact of individual vulnerabilities and strengths in determining adolescents' resilience or susceptibility to illness or disease.
- To obtain complete network data on friends and peers in two schools.

Study Design:

- Stratified sample of U.S. schools from 80 communities spanning grades 7-12 in 1994.
- All students in these schools completed in-school questionnaires between September 1994 and April 1995.
- Nationally representative sample of adolescents; approximately 200 per community.
- Oversamples of African Americans with a college-educated parent, Chinese, Cuban, Puerto Rican, and disabled adolescents; eligibility determined by responses on school questionnaire.
- Additional sample of pairs of adolescents of varying degrees of genetic relatedness, from identical twins to nonrelated adolescents living in the same household.
- Sixteen schools in which all students were selected for in-home interviews.
- 21,000 in-home adolescent interviews and 17,700 parent (usually mother) questionnaires completed between April and December 1995.
- 14,700 adolescents reinterviewed between April and August 1996.
- Contextual database aggregated at various levels constructed from extant data sources.
- Adolescent and school networks constructed from school questionnaire responses.

Questionnaire Topics:

School Administrator Wave I

- School characteristics and specialization.
- Teacher demographic and educational characteristics.
- Student attendance, performance, and educational expectations.
- Health services provision and referral.
- Disciplinary policies.

Adolescent School Questionnaire

- Demographic characteristics of the adolescent.
- Education and occupation of parents.
- Household members and information about other adolescents in the household.
- Risk-related behaviors, including smoking and drinking.
- Number of and activities with male and female friends.
- School grades and relationships with other students and teachers.
- Expectations for the future.
- Mental, physical, and emotional health.
- Involvement in exracurricular school activities and sports.

Adolescent In-home Interview-Wave I

- Majority of topics from in-school questionnaires repeated.
- Detailed relationship information about household members.
- Nonresidential biological parents.
- Activities and relationships with parents and siblings.
- Religion.
- Tobacco, alcohol, and drug use.
- Physical limitations.
- Sexual behavior and contraceptive use.
- Employment and earnings.
- Daily activities.
- Academics and experiences in school.
- Friends and romantic and sexual relationship partners.
- Delinquent behaviors, fighting, and violence.
- Physical development and pregnancy history.
- Self-esteem, self-efficacy, and experiences with suicide.

Parent Questionnaire

- Demographic and social characteristics.
- Employment, occupation, and receipt of welfare.
- Involvement in organizations and hobbies.
- Satisfaction with neighborhood.
- Marriages and marriage-like relationships.
- Current spouse or partner information.
- Knowledge of adolescent's friends and their parents.
- Health insurance coverage.
- Chronic, congenital, and inheritable illnesses and diseases.
- Relationship with adolescent.
- Perception of adolescent's school.

- Perception of adolescent's use of tobacco, alcohol, and drugs.
- Perception of adolescent's sexual behavior.

School Administrator Wave II

- Update characteristics, specialization, and disciplinary policies.
- Security measures.
- Dress codes.

Adolescent In-home Interview-Wave II

- Modified Wave I instrument.
- Expanded nutrition information.
- Sun exposure.
- Updated residential mobility, substance use, pregnancy, and employment histories.

Available Results and Data Files:

Public-use dataset containing one-half of the nationally representative in-home sample and one-half of the African American oversample (6,500 cases) is available through the Sociometrics Corp. For each adolescent respondent, the adolescent school questionnaire, the parent questionnaire, and the Wave II adolescent interview will be attached (as available). For ordering information, contact:

Sociometrics Corporation
170 State St., Suite 260
Los Altos, CA 94022-2812
Phone: (650) 949-3282
Fax: (650) 949-3299
E-mail: socio@socio.com

Contractual data will be available through the Carolina Population Center. Persons qualifying for the contractual data will receive individual datasets containing:

- 21,000 Wave I adolescent interviews with the school and parent questionnaire data attached (as available);
- 154 school administrator questionnaires Wave I;
- 128 school administrator questionnaires Wave II;
- Contextual data base (approximately 4,000 variables);
- Network dataset (approximately 400 variables); and
- 14,700 Wave II adolescent interviews.

For information regarding the contractual data, contact:

Add Health Data Support Staff
Carolina Population Center
123 West Franklin St., Room 206
Chapel Hill, NC 27516-3997
Phone: (919) 966-8412
Fax: (919) 966-7019
E-mail: addhealth@unc.edu

Plans for Future Waves:

A competing continuation will be submitted to NIH to collect a third wave of interviews from these adolescents in 2000.

Other Funding Agencies:

National Cancer Institute; National Institute of Alcohol Abuse and Alcoholism; National Institute of Deafness and Other Communication Disorders; National Institute on Drug Abuse; National Institute of General Medical Sciences; National Institute of Mental Health; National Institute of Nursing Research; Office of AIDS Research, NIH; Office of Behavioral and Social Science Research, NIH; Office of the Director, NIH; Office of Research on Women's Health, NIH; National Center for Health Statistics, Centers for Disease Control and Prevention, U.S. Department of Health and Human Services (DHHS); Office of Population Affairs, DHHS; Office of Minority Health, Centers for Disease Control and Prevention, DHHS; Office of Minority Health, Office of Public Health and Science, DHHS; Office of the Assistant Secretary for Planning and Evaluation, DHHS; and National Science Foundation.

Contact:

J. Richard Udry, Principal Investigator
University of North Carolina at Chapel Hill
Phone: (919) 966-2829
Fax: (919) 966-7019
E-mail: udry@unc.edu

Chris Bachrach, Program Officer
National Institute of Child Health and Human Development
Phone: (301) 496-1174
Fax: (301) 496-0962
E-mail: bachracc@hd01.nichd.nih.gov
The Internet address of the Add Health homepage is http://cpc.unc.edu/addhealth.

Dataset Name:	National Longitudinal Survey of Youth 1979 (NLSY79)

Sponsoring Organization:	Bureau of Labor Statistics
Data Collection Organization:	U.S. Bureau of the Census National Opinion Research Center
Principal Investigator:	Randall Olsen Center for Human Resource Research Ohio State University

Description:

The National Longitudinal Survey (NLS) was begun in the mid 1960's to collect data on the labor force experience of 20,000 participants, who were interviewed about such information as current employment status, work history, and characteristics of last job. The survey began with four samples: young men 14-24 years old as of January 1, 1966; young women 14-24 years old as of January 1, 1968; older men 45-59 years old as of January 1, 1966; and older women 30-44 years old as of January 1, 1967. In the early 1980's, the young men and older men surveys were discontinued. In 1979, a new cohort was begun with a sample of over 12,000 young men and women who were 14-21 years of age as of January 1, 1979. The survey with the addition of the new youth cohort was called the National Longitudinal Survey of Youth (NLSY) or NLSY79. This cohort has been interviewed every year since it began.

Beginning in 1986, the children of the female respondents in the NLSY79 cohort were also studied. This new cohort—called the Children and Young Adults of the NLSY79—or NLSY79 Child and Young Adults—as well as a separate, new cohort of the NLSY that began in 1997—called the NLSY97—are described elsewhere in this appendix.

Contact:

Randall Olsen
Center for Human Research
921 Chatham Lane, Suite 200
Columbus, OH 43221
Phone: (614) 442-7300
Fax: (614) 442-7329

Frank Mott
Center for Human Research
921 Chatham Lane, Suite 200
Columbus, OH 43221
Phone: (614) 442-7328
E-mail: mott@pewter.chrr.ohio-state.edu

Dataset Name:	National Longitudinal Survey of Youth 1997 (NLSY 97)
Sponsoring Organization:	Bureau of Labor Statistics
Data Collection Organization:	National Opinion Research Center
Principal Investigator:	Michael Horrigan, Program Director Bureau of Labor Statistics

Purpose:

To provide information about young people making the transition into the labor market and into adulthood, career, and family formation. The data will improve understanding of how different youths negotiate the transition and help researchers identify the antecedents and causes for youths who experience difficulties making the transition from school to work.

Design:

A representative national sample of approximately 10,000 youth 12 to 16 years old on December 31, 1996. Black and Hispanic persons will be oversampled to permit racial and ethnic comparisons.

Periodicity:

Annually. First round of interviews from February to September 1997.

Content, Policy, and Research Issues:

Data are collected on the cognitive, social, and emotional development of young people. In the initial survey both a parent and a youth interview are administered. Questions are asked about family background, marital and employment history, health, income, and assets. Both interviews have self-administered portions providing data on such issues as smoking, drinking, dating, religious beliefs, depression, and expectations. Information will also be obtained from school administrators and school transcripts. A math test will be administered to ninth graders in the survey. The Armed Services Vocational and Aptitude Battery will be used to assess respondents' aptitude, achievement, and career interests.

Contact:

Michael W. Horrigan
National Longitudinal Surveys
Suite 4945
2 Massachusetts Ave., NE
Washington, DC 20212-0011
Phone: (202) 606-7386
Fax: (202) 606-4602

Dataset Name:	New Immigrant Survey Pilot Study (NIS-PS)

Sponsoring Organizations:	National Institutes of Health U.S. Immigration and Naturalization Service National Science Foundation
Data Collection Organizations:	RAND U.S. Immigration and Naturalization Service
Principal Investigators:	Guillermina Jasso, New York University Douglas S. Massey, University of Pennsylvania Mark R. Rosenzweig, University of Pennsylvania James P. Smith, RAND

Purpose:

The NIS Pilot Study has three aims: (1) to assess the cost effectiveness of alternative methods for locating and maximizing the initial response rates of sampled immigrants; (2) to explore the costs, feasibility, and effectiveness of alternative methods of tracking over time sampled immigrants after their initial contacts that will permit a longitudinal survey of a highly mobile population with minimal attrition; and (3) to obtain immediately useful information from the NIS pilot that would both aid in the design of survey instruments for the full survey and provide new and important information on recently admitted immigrants.

Design and Periodicity:

The NIS-PS consists of a baseline survey, a three-month follow-up of half of the original sample, a six-month follow-up of all original sample members, and a one-year follow-up, also of all original sample members.

The sampling frame for the study consists of all persons who were admitted to legal permanent residence during the months of July and August 1996. The total number of immigrants admitted during this period was 148,987. Because children are quite numerous among immigrants and because employment-based immigrants, in whom there is great interest, are a relatively small category, a stratified random sample was drawn, undersampling children and oversampling the employment based. The sample thus drew 1,982 persons.

Content:

Two types of data are pertinent. The first consists of data on sociodemographic and economic characteristics and activities, so that immigrants and their children can be compared with native-born persons; examples include marital and employment histories. The second type consists of data on characteristics and behavior unique to immigrants; such data include migration and language acquisition histories.

Contact:

Guillermina Jasso, New York University, jasso@is3.nyu.edu
Douglas S. Massey, University of Pennsylvania, dmassey@lexis.pop.upenn.edu
Mark R. Rosenzweig, University of Pennsylvania, markr@markr2.pop.upenn.edu
James P. Smith, RAND Corporation, James_Smith@monty.rand.org

Dataset Name: NICHD Study of Early Child Care

Sponsoring Organization: National Institute of Child Health and
                                 Human Development (NICHD)

Data Collection Organization:

Data are collected by 10 research teams located at the University of Arkansas, Little Rock; University of California, Irvine; University of Kansas, Lawrence; Wellesley College, Wellesley, Massachusetts; University of Pittsburgh, Pittsburgh, Pennsylvania; Temple University, Philadelphia, Pennsylvania; University of Virginia, Charlottesville; University of Washington, Seattle; Western Carolina Center, Morganton, North Carolina; and University of Wisconsin, Madison.

Principal Investigator:

The principal investigator for the NICHD Study of Early Child Care is its steering committee, which consists of the principal investigators of the 10 grants for this study, the principal investigator of the grant for data coordination, the NICHD scientific project officer, and the chair of the steering committee. Members of the steering committee are Jay Belsky, Cathryn Booth, Robert Bradley, Alison Clarke-Stewart, Martha Cox, Sarah L. Friedman, Tyler Hartwell, Lewis P. Lipsitt, Marion O'Brien, Robert Pianta, Deborah Lowe Vandell, and Marsha Weinraub.

Coprincipal investigators are Virginia D. Allhusen, Celia Brownell, Donna Bryant, Peg Burchinal, Bettye Caldwell, Susan Campbell, Kathryn Hirsh-Pasek, Aletha Huston, Lyz Jaeger, Deborah Johnson, Nancy Marshall, Margaret Tresch Owen, Chris Payne, Deborah Phillips, Suzanne Randolph, Wendy Wagner-Robeson, Susan Spieker, Deborah Stipek, and Janet Ward.

Previously affiliated investigators are Mark Appelbaum, DeeAnn Batten, Kaye Fendt, and Henry Ricciuti.

Description:

The NICHD Study of Early Child Care is a natural history longitudinal study of the relationship between variations in child care and family rearing environments and the social, emotional, cognitive, linguistic, and health development of children from one month of age through first grade. An important distinguishing feature of the study is the diversity of the children and their families.

The children whose families were recruited into the study in 1991 were all full-term and healthy at birth. They came from different geographical regions across the United States, from urban and rural settings, from different socioeconomic backgrounds, family structures, and racial/cultural groups. Child care arrangements and histories also were diverse. Relative care (father care, grandparent care), in-home nonrelative care, child care homes, and child care centers are all under investigation, since the study follows the children in the care settings in which they are placed by their parents. Many children are in multiple child care arrangements concurrently and over time. The study methods include questionnaires, interviews, observation, and testing with multiple methods used to assess the same constructs. Analyses to date are either descriptive or focus on the association between child care and developmental outcomes, after taking into account family and child characteristics expected to be associated with the developmental outcomes under investigation. The study is supported by NICHD through a cooperative agreement that calls for scientific collaboration between the grantees and NICHD staff. The study was funded in two phases: Phase I, for the follow-up of children in the first three years of life, and Phase II, for the continuation of the study through age 7.

Objectives:

• To describe the characteristics and history of child care experiences of children born in the United States in the early 1990s. Experiences include age of entry into care, hours in care, stability of care, type of care, and quality of care.

• To describe the relationship between aspects of child care arrangements that can be regulated (ratio, group size, provider education, provider experience) and the actual experiences of children in child care (e.g., being treated with respect, sensitivity, and positive affect; being talked to; being read to; being cognitively enriched in other ways).

• To describe the relationship between family demographic, economic, and psychological characteristics and the choices parents make about child care (e.g., how early to place a child in child care, in what type of care to place the child, what quality of care to choose, and for how many hours per week to have the child in child care).

• To test hypotheses about the relationship between the experiences of children in child care (e.g., hours in care, quality of care) and children's developmental outcomes, after taking into account the relationship between family and child predictors of the same developmental outcomes. Developmental outcomes include self-control, compliance, social interactions with parents and peers, children's attachment to mother, cognitive development, language development, attention, school readiness, growth, and health status.

• To test hypotheses about differential relationships between child care, family characteristics, and developmental outcomes for children of different sex, age, socioeconomic, and ethnic backgrounds.

Study Design:

- Ten research sites.

The location of the 10 research sites was determined by the university affiliation of the investigators who were successful in a competition based on the
scientific merit of their research applications.

- A total of 1,364 families with newborn infants were recruited.

The 1,364 families are representative of the catchment sample of 6,191
families that were eligible to participate based on the study's inclusion criteria.
Each site enrolled 120 to 150 families.

- Longitudinal natural history study over the first seven years of children's
  life.
- An ecological theoretical model guides the investigation.

The ecological conceptualization requires in-depth cumulative assessment of
the environments in which children grow as well as assessment of their unfolding
developmental outcomes.

- Both the family and child care environments were visited, and data were
  collected about these environments using multiple measures: questionnaires, interviews, and detailed observations. Methods of assessments consisted of those
  available in the scientific literature, others that were modified for the purpose of
  the study, and new ones created specifically for this study.
- Children's behavior was assessed by observational methods and testing.
  Methods were borrowed from the scientific literature and were either used "as is"
  or modified slightly.
- Data were collected in the family environment when the children were 1,
  6, 15, 24, 36, and 54 months old and when they entered first grade (or a second
  year of preschool).
- Data were collected in child care settings when the children were 6, 15,
  24, 36, and 54 months old. Data were collected in school when the children
  entered first grade (or a second year of preschool). Kindergarten data were
  collected indirectly from parents and teachers.
- Data were collected in a laboratory setting when the children were 15, 24,
  36, and 54 months old and again when they entered first grade.

During the children's first three years of life, additional data were collected
every three months by phone interviews. Later the spacing of phone interviews

was increased first to every four months and then, following the 54-months age period, to every six months.

Constructs measured:

- Social-emotional constructs: quality of relationships, adjustment, self-concept and self-identity.
- Cognitive constructs: global intellectual functioning, knowledge and achievement, cognitive processes, language development.
- Health: growth, ear infections, intestinal problems, upper respiratory tract problems, chronic illness.
- Alternate care context: structural aspects, quantity, stability, quality, caregiver characteristics.
- Home/family context: structural context, quality of home life, parent characteristics.
- School context: structural context, school curriculum, children's perceptions.

Plans for Future Waves:

NICHD is currently in the process of evaluating the possibility of extending the study through the children's thirteenth birthdays. Early adolescence is a period of major biological and psychological transition. The extensive information that the NICHD study provides about child rearing and child development in infancy, the toddler years, and middle childhood provides a unique opportunity to study the predicted and unpredicted connections between early developmental processes and developmental outcomes in early adolescence. While the general methodological approach is likely to stay the same, new constructs and emphases will need to be added to capture the growing number of developmental issues and tasks facing adolescents.

Available Results:

Requests for papers describing results of the NICHD Study of Early Child Care should be directed to: Public Information and Communication Branch, NICHD, Bldg. 31, Room 2A32, 9000 Rockville Pike, Bethesda, MD 20892.

Future Availability of Data Files:

Data from Phase I of the study (the children's first three years of life) will be made available in January 2000.

Agencies/Organizations Involved in Planning the NICHD Study of Early Child Care:

NICHD planned the overall blueprint for the study. It determined that most of the resources will go to a common protocol and that only about 15 percent of the resources in Phase I and no resources in Phase II will go to site-specific research. NICHD has called for a sample characterized by ethnic diversity. It requires that the data will be checked and analyzed centrally, by a data coordinating center. NICHD has requested that the study will focus on developmental outcomes in multiple domains: social, emotional, cognitive, growth, and health. All other aspects of the overall research design and details of the science were planned and monitored by the steering committee for the study (which includes an NICHD investigator), with extensive input primarily from coprincipal investigators but also from site coordinators and data collectors.

The Office of Planning and Evaluation at the Department of Health and Human Services and the Administration for Children asked to extend the study in new directions (with a focus on fathers and one on Head Start-eligible children). The steering committee approved their requests and accepted additional funds to extend the study. The Foundation for Child Development added resources for analyses of the data on poor working families.

Contact:

The NICHD contact is Sarah L. Friedman, the NICHD scientific coordinator for the study and a member of its steering committee. All investigators of the NICHD Study of Early Child Care are available to talk about the study and its results.

Sarah L. Friedman, Director
Program on Cognitive, Social, and Affective Development
Child Development and Behavior Branch, NICHD
9000 Rockville Pike
Bethesda, MD 20892
Phone: (301) 496-9849
Fax: (301) 480-7773
E-mail: FriedmaS@HD01.NICHD.NIH.GOV
and SF2@CU.NIH.GOV

Dataset Name:	Panel Study of Income Dynamics (PSID) Child Development Supplement (CDS)

Sponsoring Organizations:	National Institute of Child Health and Human Development
	William T. Grant Foundation
	Annie E. Casey Foundation
	U.S. Department of Agriculture
	U.S. Department of Education
Principal Investigator:	Sandra L. Hofferth
Investigator's Institution:	University of Michigan

Purpose:

The Child Development Supplement (CDS) will add to the information gathered by the Panel Study of Income Dynamics (PSID) by collecting data on parents and their 0 to 12-year-old children. The objective is to provide researchers with a comprehensive, nationally representative, longitudinal database of children and their families with which to study the dynamic process of early human capital formation. The data collection will support studies of the way in which time, money, and social capital at the family, school, and neighborhood levels as well as parental psychological resources and sibling characteristics are linked to the cognitive and behavioral development of children. In addition, policy makers in the United States can use this information to develop and implement programs designed to promote children's health and achievement in early and middle childhood.

Description:

The PSID's existing data collection includes information dating back to 1968 on family income and work history, family structure, and neighborhood resources. In 1997 the CDS supplemented the PSID's data collection by conducting in-home interviews with 3,500 children ages 0 to 12 (including 550 immigrant children) who are children of current PSID participants. Information was also gathered from the children's parents/caregivers, teachers, and school administrators.

The study will assess children's cognitive development and find out how children spend their time in a typical day. From parents, information will be obtained about their child's health and development, child care and education, and weekly activities. Parents will also be asked about their neighborhood, types of social support available, and expectations for their children. Teachers will be asked about children's behavior and successes in their care and education programs. Additionally, school administrators will be asked to provide information about the programs and resources available in their schools.

The study began in 1997 and will follow the children through adolescence and into adulthood. The sample has been oversampled for African Americans.

Contact:

Sandra L. Hofferth
Institute of Social Research
University of Michigan
426 Thompson St.
Room 3234
Ann Arbor, MI 48106
Phone: (313) 763-5131
E-mail: hofferth@umich.edu

Dataset Name:	Program of Research on the Causes and Correlates of Delinquency
Sponsoring Institutions:	Office of Juvenile Justice and Delinquency Prevention National Institute on Drug Abuse National Institute of Mental Health The John D. and Catherine T. MacArthur Foundation
Data Collection Organization:	Surveys/data collection conducted by trained field staff of each project.
Principal Investigators:	David Huizinga (Denver study) Terrence Thornberry (Rochester study) Rolf Loeber (Pittsburgh study)

Purpose:

There is great interest in knowing how and why boys and girls become delinquent, especially serious and violent delinquents and problem drug users, and in what can be done to prevent these behaviors. Delinquency and drug use are among the most resilient forms of problem behaviors. There is a large cost to society in terms of human injury and suffering, property damage, and economic loss caused by serious delinquency. Despite our efforts as a society, we have clearly failed to limit and control delinquency. Part of this failure must be attributed to a lack of clear understanding of the causes of delinquency, so it is crucially important to better understand this behavior if it is to be successfully reduced.

In announcing this program of research, the Office of Juvenile Justice and Delinquency Prevention (OJJDP) challenged the research community to approach creatively the "why" of the development of delinquent behavior in order to provide a sound empirical basis for developing improved strategies for delinquency prevention and establishment of interdisciplinary teams to investigate the multicausal nature of antisocial behavior, including community, family, school, and individual difference influences.

Description:

There is some general agreement that one of the most appropriate ways to obtain a better understanding of delinquency and drug use is to conduct longitudinal studies that follow the same children and youth over extended periods of their lives. In this way developmental pathways and salient factors that increase the probability of successful lives and reduce serious delinquency and drug use can be understood. It is against this background that the OJJDP launched the Program of Research on the Causes and Correlates of Delinquency. This program involves three coordinated projects: Denver Youth Survey (University of Colorado), Pittsburgh Youth Study (University of Pittsburgh), and Rochester Youth Development Study (University of Albany).

Among the salient features of the program are the following:

- It includes three highly coordinated longitudinal projects, so key findings can be replicated and cross-validated.
- The three research teams collaborated extensively in the design of the studies, identification of key theoretical constructs, and development of "core" measures of these constructs.
- The studies have a large representation of minorities and include both boys and girls.
- Using accelerated longitudinal designs at two sites, the studies cover a large age span, currently ages 7 to 24.
- The studies maintain frequent contact and interview assessments with respondents (six-month or annual interviews).
- The studies have maintained high retention rates: over 90 percent in the first five years, and over 80 percent during years six through eight.

Objectives:

- Epidemiology and cooccurrence of delinquency, drug use, and other problem behaviors over the life course.
- Understanding delinquent careers: onset, duration, termination; causal factors associated with initiation, maintenance, escalation, and termination.
- Identifying developmental pathways through multiple contexts from childhood through early adulthood that lead to successful outcomes or serious delinquency.
- Examining whether delinquency, drug use, and other antisocial behaviors are a single phenomenon, or whether they are distinctly different antisocial outcomes with different sets of causal factors.
- Providing information about the timing and nature of successful prevention and intervention strategies.

Study Design:

- Three coordinated projects.
- Baseline: face-to-face interviews in private settings with child/youth respondents and a principal caretaker.
- Semiannual or annual face-to-face follow-ups (supplemented by telephone interviews for those at a distance from study sites).

- Respondents: 4,544 children and youth, ages 7-15 in 1987 and a principal caretaker.
- Archival data from police, courts, schools, and social services.
- Oversample of youth at high risk for serious delinquency.

Interview Schedule Topics:

- Child and adolescent problem behavior: delinquency and violent behavior (self-reports and official reports), drug use/abuse, gang membership, psychopathology, victimization, and sexual behavior and pregnancy.
- Child and adolescent characteristics/experiences: employment, attachment to family, involvement in conventional activities, attitudes toward delinquent behavior, impulsiveness, religion, other.
- Family variables: family demographics (family structure, occupation, education, income of parents), child supervision and monitoring, discipline style and practices, family life events, marital discord/violence.
- School variables: academic attendance and achievement, commitment/ attachment to school, involvement in school activities.
- Peer variables: involvement with delinquent peers, involvement with drug-using peers, involvement with conventional peers.
- Neighborhood variables: neighborhood economic and physical characteristics, cultural heterogeneity, neighborhood crime and deviance, neighborhood illegitimate opportunities.
- Use of mental health services (by family members and individual respondent).

Plans for Future Waves:

All three projects are ongoing. The Rochester project anticipates continuing into 1998-2002, with the children born to the original youth respondents of the survey becoming a part of the future survey years. The Denver and Pittsburgh projects are ongoing through 1999 and may continue later.

Available Results and Data Files:

Results are available in several annual and special reports from the Office of Juvenile Justice and Delinquency Prevention (OJJDP), 633 Indiana Ave., NW, Washington, DC 20531. A sequence of publications (*Youth Development Series*) that contain program findings has also been initiated by the OJJDP. Results are also available from the individual projects and in several academic publications.

Planning for procedures and format of public release data files from the program is in process. Collaborative efforts with other researchers using program data in conjunction with other longitudinal datasets are in process.

Contact:

Program Information:
David Huizinga
Institute of Behavioral Science
810 7th St., NW
Boulder, CO 80303
Phone: (303) 492-1266
Fax: (303) 449-8479

Denver Study:
David Huizinga, PI (see above)

Pittsburgh Study:
Rolf Loeber, PI
Life History Studies
University of Pittsburgh
3811 O'Hara St.
Pittsburgh, PA 15213
Phone: (412) 383-1015
Fax: (412) 383-1112

Rochester Study:
Terrence Thornberry, PI
School of Criminal Justice
University of Albany
135 Western Ave.
Albany, NY 12222
Phone: (518) 442-5218
Fax: (518) 442-5603

Dataset Name:	Project on Human Development in Chicago Neighborhoods
Sponsoring Organizations:	The John D. and Catherine T. MacArthur Foundation National Institute of Justice National Institute of Mental Health
Principal Investigator:	Felton Earls
Coprincipal Investigator:	Stephen Buka
Investigators' Institution:	Harvard University

Purpose:

The Project on Human Development in Chicago Neighborhoods is designed to offer a comprehensive understanding of human development and social behavior, with particular attention to the multilevel causes and effects of social competence versus antisocial behavior. The study will enhance current knowledge on factors leading to some of the nation's most serious public health problems, including delinquency, criminal behavior, violence, and substance abuse. In addition, the study will provide important new information about a major urban area, Chicago, in the 1990s.

Perhaps, most important, information generated by the study will help build a rational foundation for urgently needed policy decisions. The study's findings can point the way to a more coordinated approach to social development and its failures—an approach that involves families, schools, communities, and public institutions working together. The findings can help policy makers make more effective use of limited resources in promoting social competence and designing new strategies for preventive intervention, treatment, rehabilitation, and sanctions.

Design:

The Project on Human Development in Chicago Neighborhoods studies both the effect of the community on the individual and the effect of the individual on the community. The study will look at the individual in the context of family, peers, school, neighborhood, and community, using an interdisciplinary point of view, combining observations and insights from such fields as psychiatry, psychology, sociology, criminology, public health, medicine, education, human behavior, and statistics.

The Project on Human Development in Chicago Neighborhoods is essentially two studies in one. The first component is the community design, which employs four data collection approaches to characterize neighborhoods across

Chicago: (1) a community survey (CS) of 8,500 Chicago residents, (2) a systematic social observation component, (3) a neighborhood experts' survey of 3,000 key neighborhood representatives, and (4) a variety of agency and administrative datasets. These are designed to acquire information concerning social, economic, organizational, political, and cultural structures; formal and informal social control; and social cohesion of Chicago neighborhoods. The project used data from the 1990 Census to split Chicago into 343 neighborhood clusters. Information was gathered on all 343 neighborhood clusters through interviews with households and key community members, systematic observations of the communities' physical and social characteristics, and official records.

The second component is the Longitudinal Cohort Study (LCS). Using an accelerated longitudinal design, the LCS will follow children and youth as they move through childhood and adolescence into adulthood. From 1995 to 2003, field interviews will be conducted annually in English, Spanish, and Polish with the help of computer-assisted interviewing. The approximately 7,000 participants in the LCS were chosen from 80 randomly selected, representative neighborhoods and split into seven cohorts (children and youth ages 0-1, 3, 6, 9, 12, 15, and 18 in 1996). Participants have been drawn from a balanced representation of African American, Latino, white, and mixed communities and from all social classes in each ethnic group.

In 1994, an infant study was added that will follow the development of 400 infants who were between 5 and 7 months old in 1994.

Contact:

Stephen Buka
Assistant Professor
Harvard School of Public Health
677 Huntington Ave.
Boston, MA 02115-6028
Phone: (617) 432-1080

Dataset Name:	Survey of Program Dynamics for Assessing Welfare Reform (SPD)

Sponsoring Institution:	U.S. Bureau of the Census
Data Collection Organization:	U.S. Bureau of the Census
Principal Investigators:	Michael McMahon and Daniel H. Weinberg U.S. Bureau of the Census

Purpose:

To collect data on the demographic, social, and economic characteristics of a nationally representative sample of the U.S. population in order to evaluate recent federal welfare reform legislation and its impact on the American people. These data will provide the basis for an overall evaluation of how well welfare reforms are achieving the aims of the Clinton administration and the Congress and meeting the needs of the American people.

Survey Design and Sample Size:

Congress mandated that the Census Bureau continue to collect data on the 1992 and 1993 panels of the Survey of Income and Program Participation (SIPP) as necessary to obtain information on changes in program participation, employment, earnings, and measures of adult and child well-being through the SPD. The data collected from the 1992 and 1993 SIPP panels provide three years of longitudinal baseline data prior to major welfare reform. Data collected in these panels include program eligibility, access and participation, transfer income and in-kind benefits, detailed economic and demographic data on employment and job transitions, income, and family composition. The three years of SIPP data combined with the six years of SPD data collection will provide panel data for up to 10 years (1992-2001).

The SPD survey has three phases:

The Bridge Survey. This survey was used to collect income and program participation data in the spring of 1997 for calendar year 1996 from the SPD sample. The Bridge Survey allowed investigators to recontact the interviewed sample persons in the 1992 and 1993 SIPP panels and bring them back into the sample for the SPD. To collect these data, investigators used a modified version of the March 1997 Current Population Survey (CPS), since the data collected from the CPS income supplement are similar to the data to be collected in the 1998 SPD. The Bridge Survey also included additional questions to obtain data not collected for 1995 from the 1992 SIPP panel. The sample size was approximately 35,000 households, which included all persons interviewed in the last wave who were also interviewed in the first wave of the 1992 and 1993 SIPP panels. Successful interviews were obtained from approximately 82 percent of eligible households.

1998 SPD including a 1997 pretest. The second phase of the SPD is full implementation of the core SPD questionnaire developed in 1995 with a supplemental self-administered adolescent questionnaire. Information on these sample persons will be obtained using a computer-assisted SPD instrument, with annual recall for the preceding calendar year. The SPD instrument includes a set of retrospective questions for all persons 15 and older that focus on such topics as jobs, income, and program participation. Additional questions on children in the household will gather information on school status, activities at home, child care, health care, and child support. A few additional questions will be asked for sample persons who moved prior to the Bridge Survey and with whom an interview could not be obtained during 1997. The self-administered adolescent questionnaire will obtain information from persons 12 to 17 years of age using an audio cassette-administered instrument. A pretest was conducted for the 1998 SPD in October 1997 using a sample of 400 retired March 1996 CPS households in four of the Census Bureau's regional offices. The sample for the 1998 SPD will be approximately 17,500 households. Subsampling plans will focus on retaining households with children at the low end of the income distribution.

1999 SPD and later. The third phase of the SPD is the 1999 SPD, which will include a topical module focusing on issues pertaining to children's well-being as well as the core SPD questionnaire instrument. Topics are being identified for the topical module and a decision on the content will be made in the next few months.

Type of Respondent:

A household respondent, who must be a knowledgeable household member at least 15 years old, provides information for each household member.

Sponsoring Agency and Legal Authorities:

The Census Bureau conducts the survey under the authority of the Personal Responsibility and Work Opportunity Reconciliation Act of 1996 (Public Law 104-193), Section 414.

Periodicity:

A longitudinal survey conducted on a yearly basis, with interviewing planned for April through June.

Release of Results:

The Census Bureau will collect and process the data to create a public-use microdata file.

Historical Background:

P.L. 104-193 requires and funds a new survey by the Census Bureau, the Survey of Program Dynamics (SPD), to "continue to collect data on the 1992 and 1993 panels of the Survey of Income and Program Participation (SIPP) as necessary to obtain such information as will enable interested persons to evaluate the impact [of the law] on a random national sample of recipients of assistance under state programs funded under this part and (as appropriate) other low-income families, and in doing so, shall pay particular attention to the issues of out-of-wedlock birth, welfare dependency, the beginning and end of welfare spells, and the causes of repeat welfare spells, and shall obtain information about the status of children participating in such panels."

Special Features:

The survey meets a specific need, to evaluate the effects of the 1996 welfare reforms, not currently addressed by other surveys.

Future Outlook:

Plans are to conduct this survey through the year 2002 to collect data that will enable interested persons to evaluate the 1996 federal welfare reform legislation and its impact on the American people.

Contact:

Michael McMahon
SPD Operations Manager
Demographic Surveys Division
Washington, DC 20233-8400
Phone: (301) 457-3819
Fax: (301) 457-2306
E-mail: Michael.F.McMahon@census.gov

Dataset Name:	Wisconsin Longitudinal Study (WLS)
Data Collection Organization:	University of Wisconsin
Principal Investigator:	Robert M. Hauser
Investigator's Institution:	Center for Demography University of Wisconsin, Madison

Description:

The Wisconsin Longitudinal Study (WLS) is a long-term study of a random sample of 10,317 men and women who graduated from Wisconsin high schools in 1957. Survey data were collected from the original respondents or their parents in 1957, 1964, 1975, and 1992 and from a selected sibling in 1977 and 1993. These data provide a full record of social background, youthful aspirations, schooling, military service, family formation, labor market experiences, and social participation of the original respondents. The survey data from earlier years have been supplemented by mental ability tests (of primary respondents and 2,000 of their siblings), measures of school performance, and characteristics of communities of residence, schools and colleges, employers, and industries. The WLS records for primary respondents are also linked to those of three same-sex high school friends in the study population. Social background measures include earnings histories of parents from Wisconsin state tax records. In 1977 the study design was expanded with the collection of parallel interview data for a highly stratified subsample of 2,000 siblings of the primary respondents. In the 1992-1993 round of the WLS, the sample was expanded to include a randomly selected sibling of every respondent (with at least one brother or sister), and the content was extended to obtain detailed occupational histories and job characteristics; incomes, assets, and interhousehold transfers; social and economic characteristics of parents, siblings, and children and descriptions of the respondents' relationships with them; and extensive information about mental and physical health and well-being.

The WLS cohort of men and women, born mainly in 1939, precedes by about a decade the bulk of the baby boom generation that continues to tax social institutions and resources at each stage of life. For this reason, the study can provide early indications of trends and problems that will become important as the larger group passes through its fifties. This adds to the value of the study in obtaining basic information about the life course as such, independent of the cohort's vanguard position with respect to the baby boom generation. In addition, the WLS is also the first of the large longitudinal studies of American adolescents and thus provides the first large-scale opportunity to study the life course from late adolescence through the mid-50s in the context of a complete record of ability, aspiration, and achievement.

Design:

The WLS sample is broadly representative of white non-Hispanic American men and women who have at least a high school education. Among Americans ages 50 to 54 in 1990 and 1991, approximately 66 percent are non-Hispanic white persons who completed at least 12 years of schooling. The sample is mainly of German, English, Irish, Scandinavian, Polish, or Czech ancestry. Some strata of American society are not well represented. Everyone in the primary sample graduated from high school; about 7 percent of their siblings did not. It has been estimated that about 75 percent of Wisconsin youth graduated from high school in the late 1950s. Minorities are not well represented; there are only a handful of African American, Hispanic, or Asian persons in the sample; given the longitudinal design of the WLS and the miniscule numbers of minorities in Wisconsin at the time the study began, there is no way to remedy this omission. About 19 percent of the WLS sample is of farm origin, which is consistent with national estimates of persons of farm origin in cohorts born in the late 1930s. As in the later large longitudinal studies of school-based samples, age variation occurs in repeated observations, rather than in cross-section. Also, siblings cover several adjoining cohorts; they were mainly born between 1930 and 1948. In 1964, in 1975, and again in 1992, about two-thirds of the sample lived in Wisconsin and about one-third lived elsewhere in the United States or abroad.

Investigators have completed the 1992-1993 follow-up survey of about 9,000 men and women who were first interviewed as seniors in Wisconsin high schools in 1957 and were subsequently followed up in 1957, 1964, and 1975; most respondents were 53 or 54 years old when interviewed. Also interviewed here were other members of the original sample who were not interviewed in 1975 (475 of 850 surviving nonrespondents). In all, 8,493 of the 9,741 surviving members of the original sample have been interviewed. Selected siblings of the high school graduates also have been randomly interviewed. Some 2,000 siblings were previously interviewed in 1977; they and approximately 2,800 more siblings have been interviewed in this round of the study. The surveys included a one-hour telephone interview, followed by a 20-page self-administered questionnaire. Brief close-out interviews have been carried out with a relative of each respondent who has died, and, in cases where the selected sibling has died, close-out data have been obtained from the original respondent.

Available Results and Data Files:

These new follow-up data, linked with existing files, are a valuable public resource for studies of aging and the life course, intergenerational transfers and relationships, family functioning, social stratification, physical and mental well-being, and mortality. In the future the value of the sample and the data will be enhanced with additional data linkages, specifically, to locate high school test scores for brothers and sisters of primary respondents and death certificates for deceased primary respondents.

Documentation, publication lists, and modular public-use data files from the WLS are available from the Data and Program Library Services Web-site (http://dpls.dacc.wisc.edu/WLS/). In addition, a program (WLSGV) is provided for VMS, PC, and UNIX platforms that will generate code in SPSS or SAS to extract variables and merge data from different modules.

Additional source materials about the WLS are available from the Center for Demography and Ecology, University of Wisconsin-Madison, 1180 Observatory Dr., Madison, WI 53706, or by e-mail at cdepubs@ssc.wisc.edu. For additional information about the WLS, send e-mail to wls@ssc.wisc.edu.

Public releases of the WLS data are also available from DPLS:

Data and Program Library Services
University of Wisconsin-Madison
3313 Social Sciences Bldg.
1180 Observatory Dr.
Madison, WI 53706
Phone: (608) 262-7962
Fax: (608) 262-4747
E-mail: dpls@dpls.dacc.wisc.edu
WWW: http://dpls.dacc.wisc.edu

APPENDIX
B

Survey Characteristics

TABLE B-1 Survey Characteristics

Survey	Sample	Oversamples	Planned Periodicity	Major Topics
British National Child Development Study (NCDS)	All persons born the week March 3-9, 1958, in Great Britain, about 16,500 total. In 1991 all children of a random sample of one-third of NCDS respondents (age 33) were added.	None	Five major follow-ups since 1958: • 1965 (7 years old). • 1969 (11 years old). • 1974 (16 years old). • 1981 (23 years old). • 1991 (33 years old.	Factors associated with birth outcomes. Family formation, employment, education, training, housing, income, health, smoking, drinking, voluntary activities. Children's cognitive, socio-emotional, and behavioral outcomes.

Contexts Studied	Planned Linkage Capacities	Incentive Given?	Type of Data Collection	Informatio Contact (as of 2/98)
Family, school, community.	Census data; school records.		Interviews with parents, teachers, spouses, cohabitees, children.	John Bynner Peter Shepherd NCDS User Support Social Statistics Research Unit
			Medical exams.	City University Northampton Square
			Educational tests.	London ECIV QHB
			Mother, children, mother figure.	Phone: (0171) 477-8484 Fax: (0171) 477-8583 E-mail: ncds@ssru.city.ac.uk

TABLE B-1   Continued

Survey	Sample	Oversamples	Planned Periodicity	Major Topics
Canadian National Longitudinal Survey of Children and Youth (NLSCY)	National sample of 22,831 children ages 0 to 11 in 1994 from 13,439 households in the 10 provinces (excludes Yukon and Northwest territories). (Data for Northwest and Yukon territories will be analyzed separately.) Cohorts: 0-11 months, 1 year, 2-3 years, 4-5 years, 6-7 years, 8-9 years, 10-11 years old. As the children grow older, new children ages 0-2 will be added to the sample.	Households that contained at least one child in the two youngest cohorts.	Study began in 1994; children surveyed every two years into adulthood. Cycle 1: • household collection, November 1994 to June 1995. • school collection, March to June 1995. Cycle 2: • household collection, November 1996 to April 1997. • school collection, March to June 1997.	Child development.

Contexts Studied	Planned Linkage Capacities	Incentive Given?	Type of Data Collection	Information Contact (as of 2/98)
Parent(s). Family. School. Neighborhood.	Currently no planned linkages.	No incentive given.	In-home: • face-to-face or telephone interviews. • main respondent is "person most knowledgeable" about the child, usually the mother. • 4-5 year olds tested face to face for school readiness. • 10-11 year olds completed self-administered questionnaire. In Cycle 2, 12-13 year olds also completed self-administered questionnaire. In-school (for school-age cohorts): • teachers and principals completed questionnaires sent by mail. • teachers administered math tests (also sent by mail) to children in grade 2 and above; in Cycle 2 a reading comprehension test was added.	Gilles Montigny Statistics Canada Tunney's Pasture Ottawa, Ontario Canada K1A0T6 Phone: (613) 951-9731

TABLE B-1   Continued

Survey	Sample	Oversamples	Planned Periodicity	Major Topics
Children and Young Adults of the National Longitudinal Surveys of Youth	All children born to female participants in the NLSY79 cohort interviewed in 1986; in addition, all children born since 1986 who reside at least part-time with their mothers. Starting in 1994, children 15 and older at date of interview in the household within the previous 2 rounds were interviewed regardless of current residence status. In 1986, 5,255 children; 4,971 assessed. In 1988, 6,543 children; 6,266 assessed. In 1990, 6,427 children; 5,803 assessed. In 1992, 7,255 children; 6,599 assessed. In 1994, 6,622 children not young adults; 6,109 assessed. In 1994, 1,240 young adult children; 980 interviewed.	None.	Began in 1986; assessments are conducted biennially of both mothers and children. Since 1988, children ages 10 and over also complete a confidential self-report in addition to assessments. Starting in 1994 (and each subsequent round), children ages 15 or older as of Dec. 31 of the survey year receive a comprehensive omnibus questionnaire in lieu of assessments.	Linkages between maternal-family behaviors and attitudes and subsequent child development.

Contexts Studied	Planned Linkage Capacities	Incentive Given?	Type of Data Collection	Information Contact (as of 2/98)
Family. Job. School. Cognitive, socio-emotional, and physiological development of each child.	Current link between child interviews and 1995 NLSY79 Child School Survey file for children 5 and older. Current link to QED data for schools identified in 1995 NLSY79 Child School Survey. Planned links to geocode data files and files on neighborhood characteristics.		Paper-and-pencil personal interviews administered by National Opinion Research Center interviewers. Self-reports from older children and mothers. Starting in 1994, computer assisted personal interviews (CAPI) used for child assessments and young adult interviews. School transcripts and student and principal questionnaires used in 1995 Child School Survey.	Randall Olsen Director Center for Human Resource Research 921 Chatham Lane Columbus, OH 43221 Phone: (614) 442-7300 E-mail: stats.bls.gov:80/ nlsmothr.html

TABLE B-1   Continued

Survey	Sample	Oversamples	Planned Periodicity	Major Topics
Delinquency in a Birth Cohort in the People's Republic of China	5,341 males and females born in 1973.		Study began in 1990; will continue until 2000.	Delinquency, school records. occupation, income, marital status, age, sex, family.
Early Childhood Longitudinal Study • Birth Cohort 2000 (ECLS-B) *(NOTE: This study is still in the development stages; certain details have not been finalized).*	Nationally representative sample of approximately 15,000 children born during 2000. Racially/ethnically and socio-economically diverse.	Asian and Pacific Islanders. Maybe other minorities, such as Native Americans. Also maybe high-risk children (low-birth weight, low-income).	Study of children from birth through grade 1: • first data collection occurs within 6 months of birth, followed by data collections at 12, 18, and 24 or 30 months. • Thereafter, data will be collected on a roughly annual basis (exact timing to be determined).	Children's early learning and development, specifically: • development and growth, • transition to non-parental care and school, • school readiness.

Contexts Studied	Planned Linkage Capacities	Incentive Given?	Type of Data Collection	Information Contact (as of 2/98)
School, family, community.	School records, census, police files.		Interviews with subjects, parents, teachers. control group.	Department of Criminology University of Pennsylvania 3937 Chestnut St. Philadelphia, PA 19104-3110
Homes/family. Communities. Child care. Early childhood program environments. Schools. Classrooms. Teachers. Children's physical, social, emotional, and cognitive development.	ZIP codes, census codes.	Age-appropriate gifts to children (e.g., children's books). Whether monetary incentives will be given to parents and child care providers has not yet been determined.	Primary source of information: interviews with parents (usually mother, as primary caretaker). In addition: • direct assessments of children's cognitive and non-cognitive development beginning at 2 1/2 years of age. • interviews with child care providers/ teachers. • when children reach school age, school administrators and teachers to complete questionnaire.	Jerry West National Center for Education Statistics 555 New Jersey Ave., NW, Room 417B Washington, DC 20208 Phone: (202) 219-1574 E-mail: Jerry_West@ED.GOV ECLS@ED.GOV

TABLE B-1   Continued

Survey	Sample	Oversamples	Planned Periodicity	Major Topics
Early Childhood Longitudinal Study • Kindergarten Class of 1998-99 (ECLS-K) *(NOTE: This study is still in development stages; certain details have not been finalized).*	Nationally representative sample of approximately 23,000 children enrolled in 1,000 public and private kindergartens for the 1998-99 school year. Racially/ethnically and socio-economically diverse. Will also gather information on the kindergartens that the children attend: (includes full- and part-day kindergarten programs).	Private schools and children. Asian and Pacific Islander children. (Maybe also children with disabilities.)	Information collected twice during base year (once at beginning and once at end of 1998-99 school year). Follow-ups are planned for spring of grades 1, 3, and 5. A fall grade 1 follow-up is being planned for a 25% sample of the base-year sample (approximately 5,000 children).	Children's development and environment, specifically: • school readiness • transition to school • schooling and performance in the early grades • interaction of school, family, and community.

Contexts Studied	Planned Linkage Capacities	Incentive Given?	Type of Data Collection	Information Contact (as of 2/98)
Interaction between: • child and family, • child and school, • family and school and community. Also, children's cognitive, social, and emotional growth.		$100 honorarium to schools. Teachers are paid as data collectors to report on academic achievement, social skills, and special education services ($5 per completed case). Children are given stickers and other age-appropriate gifts (e.g., children's books).	Information collected from children, parents, teachers, school, classroom, special education teachers, administrators/children's principals. Only kindergartners and first graders participate in the assessment. Beginning in grade 3, children are assessed and interviewed.	Jerry West National Center for Education Statistics 555 New Jersey Ave., NW, Room 417 Washington, DC 20208 Phone: (202) 219-1574 headmasters/ E-mail: Jerry_West@ED.GOV ECLS@ED.GOV

TABLE B-1   Continued

Survey	Sample	Oversamples	Planned Periodicity	Major Topics
Early Head Start Research and Evaluation Project	National sample of approximately 3,000 low-income families from diverse EHS programs in 17 communities (selected from 143 programs funded in 1995 and 1996). As families are recruited by programs, they are randomly assigned to the EHS program or to a comparison group. Sample members at intake are pregnant women or mothers with infants 12 months of age or younger.	None	Age-based child assessment, parent interview, and child care provider assessment when child is 14, 24, and 36 months old. Intake-based parent interview about services parent uses at 6, 15, 24, and 36 months after random assignment. Site visits in 1996,1997, and 1999	Effectiveness of EHS programs with varying approaches to affecting child and family outcomes (theories of change), in terms of: • children's cognitive, language, and social development, health, resiliency, and parental attachment; • family development, including parent-child relationships, home environment, family functioning, family health, parental involvement, and parental self-sufficiency; • staff development; and • community development, including child care quality, collaboration, and services integration.

Contexts Studied	Planned Linkage Capacities	Incentive Given?	Type of Data Collection	Information Contact (as of 2/98)
Relationships and interactions among all of the following: child, parent(s), sibling(s), Early Head Start program staff, child care providers, and communities in which EHS families live and work.	National evaluation data to be linked with data collected by 15 local researchers. Potential links to other studies of current policy relevance, including welfare reform, low-income fathers, child care, and children with disabilities. ECLS Birth Cohort.	Age-based assessments: $15 plus small gift. Intake-based interview: $10.	Data from program application and enrollment forms. Parent interviews. Direct child assessments. Observations of child care provider settings. Videotaping of mother-child interactions (at 14 and 24 months). Surveys of program staff. Site visits to programs that include interviews with all staff, observations of child development services (center and home-based), focus groups with parents, and focus groups with community representatives.	John M. Love, Program Director Mathematica Policy Research, Inc. P.O. Box 2393 Princeton, NJ 08543 Phone: (609) 275-2245 Email: jlove@ mathematica-mpr.com and Helen H. Raikes, Program Monitor Administration on Children, Youth, and Families 330 C St. SW Room 2411 Washington, DC 20011 Phone: (202) 205-2247 E-mail: heraikes@acf.dhhs.gov

TABLE B-1   Continued

Survey	Sample	Oversamples	Planned Periodicity	Major Topics
National Education Longitudinal Study (NELS:1988)	National sample of 26,435 eighth graders in 1988 attending 1,057 public and private schools.	Hispanic students. Asian/ Pacific Islander students. Subsamples (for each student): • one parent, • one school principal, • two teachers.	In 1988. Follow-up surveys in 1990, 1992, and 1994. Another follow-up proposed for 2000.	"Educational attainment": • reasons for and consequences of academic success and failure.

Contexts Studied	Planned Linkage Capacities	Incentive Given?	Type of Data Collection	Information Contact (as of 2/98)
Family. School. Classroom. Community.	ZIP codes, census codes, Integrated Postsecondary Data Education System (IPEDS).		Sample survey. School transcript records. Assessment test. In base year, first and second follow-ups: • four cognitive tests • student, parent, teacher, school administrator questionnaires. Follow-up surveys also include dropout questionnaires.	Jeffrey Owings Data Development and Longitudinal Studies Group National Center for Education Statistics 555 New Jersey Ave., NW, Room 417 Washington, DC 20208-5651 Phone: (202) 219-1777

TABLE B-1   Continued

Survey	Sample	Oversamples	Planned Periodicity	Major Topics
National Longitudinal Study of Adolescent Health (Add Health)	Clustered, school-based. WAVE I: • 90,000 seventh through twelfth grade students from 134 schools (high schools and their "feeder" schools) took in-school questionnaire. • 12,105 youth chosen for in-home interviews (approximately 200 from each pair of schools). • Genetic sample: siblings in same household. WAVE II: Included all those in WAVE I except: • students who were in grade 12 in WAVE I and did not qualify for genetic sample, • WAVE I disabled sample (was unreliable), • 65 adolescents who were not interviewed in WAVE I but qualified as part of the genetic sample.	1,038 African Americans from well-educated families (parent has college degree). 334 Chinese adolescents 450 Cuban adolescents 437 Puerto Rican adolescents	In-home interviews: • WAVE I conducted between April and December 1995. • WAVE II conducted between April and August 1996. School administrator survey: • conducted in first year of study. • updated by phone in spring 1996.	Differential health of adolescents.

Contexts Studied	Planned Linkage Capacities	Incentive Given?	Type of Data Collection	Information Contact (as of 2/98)
Social environment (from family to community). Health-related behaviors. Vulnerabilities and strengths. Family. Friends/peers. School. Neighborhood. Community.			In-school adolescent questionnaire. In-home adolescent interviews. School administrator questionnaire. Parent questionnaire. Community contextual dataset. In-school friendship network dataset. Geographic location of household in community.	J. Richard Udry Carolina Population Center University of North Carolina University Square Chapel Hill, NC 27516 Phone: (919) 966-2829 Website: www.cpc.unc.edu/ projects/addhealth/ whois.html

TABLE B-1   Continued

Survey	Sample	Oversamples	Planned Periodicity	Major Topics
National Longitudinal Survey of Youth, 1979 (NLSY:79)	12,686 youth ages 14-21 as of January 1, 1979. Dropped to 11,607 in 1985 when interviewing of military sample discontinued.	African Americans. . Hispanics. Economically disadvantaged non-African-Americans and non-Hispanics (discontinued in 1990). Youth in the military (discontinued in 1984) (women were an oversample within the youth in the military oversample).	Annual since 1979.	Labor force experience. Factors affecting labor market behavior.
National Longitudinal Survey of Youth, 1997 (NLSY:97)	12,000 youth ages 12-17. 2,500 disabled children ages 12-17.	None.	Initial interviews conducted January to May 1997. Annual interviews in following years.	Youths' transition into: • labor market, • adulthood, • career and family formation.

Contexts Studied	Planned Linkage Capacities	Incentive Given?	Type of Data Collection	Information Contact (as of 2/98)
Education/training.			Personal interviews.	Randall Olsen Director
Location.			Telephone interviews in 1987.	Center for Human Resource Research
Parents.				921 Chatham Lane Columbus, OH 43221
Marital status.				Phone: (614) 442-7300
Financial.				
Work-related attitudes.				
Health problems.				
Discrimination.				
Individual.			Computer-assisted personal field interviews of youth and parents.	Michael Horrigan Program Director National Longitudinal Surveys
Parents.				
Schools.			Self-administered audio CASI section.	Two Massachusetts Ave., NE, Suite 4945 Washington, DC 20212 Phone: (202) 606-7386
			Youth in grade 9 and below will also take a Peabody Individual Achievement math test (PIAT).	
			Survey of school administrators.	
			School transcripts.	

TABLE B-1   Continued

Survey	Sample	Oversamples	Planned Periodicity	Major Topics
New Immigrant Survey Pilot Study (NIS-PS)	1,982 child and adult (out of 148,987) immigrants who were granted legal permanent residence (PR) during July and August 1996.	Immigrants receiving PR based on employment. Undersample: children (people under the age of 18).	Baseline survey, conducted in 1997. Three-month follow-up of half the sample. Six-month follow-up of whole sample. One-year follow-up of whole sample.	Assess immigrants' experience in and adaptation to the U.S. (e.g., socioeconomic integration). Comparison of immigrants with native born. Effects of immigration on the U.S.

Contexts Studied	Planned Linkage Capacities	Incentive Given?	Type of Data Collection	Information Contact (as of 2/98)
Socio-demographic and economic characteristics and activities (to compare immigrants to native born). Characteristics and behavior unique to immigrants.			Interviews with adults (ages 18 and over). Interviews with parents or care givers of children (under age 18).	Guillermina Jasso New York University E-mail: jasso@is3nyu.edu Douglas S. Massey University of Pennsylvania E-mail: dmassey@ lexis.pop.upenn.edu Mark R. Rosenzweig University of Pennsylvania E-mail: markr@ markr2.pop.upenn.edu James P. Smith RAND Corporation E-mail: James_Smith@ monty.rand.org

TABLE B-1   Continued

Survey	Sample	Oversamples	Planned Periodicity	Major Topics
National Institute of Child Health and Human Development (NICHD) Study of Early Child Care Two components: Phase I Phase II (Phase I follow-up)	Phase I: National sample of 1,364 families; selected from designated hospitals at the 10 data collection sites; included only families with full-term healthy newborns; 123-150 participant families at each site. During child's first year: • 53% of mothers worked/went to school full-time, • 23% worked/went to school part-time, • 24% stayed home. Ethnicity of mother: • 81% white, • 19% minorities (African American, Native American, Asian, Hispanic, Mixed). Homes: • 86% two parents, • 14% single parent. Mother's education: • 11 % <grade 12, • 25% high school/GED, • 28% some college, • 24% B.A., • 12% postgrad. Phase II: Includes 1,247 families of original 1,364.	None.	Phase I: • Families recruited between January and November 1991. • Children enrolled at 1 month old were studied until 3 years old. • At 1, 6, 15, 24, and 36 months old, home visits. • At 15, 24, and 36 months old, lab setting assessment. • At 6, 15, 24, and 36 months old, observed in primary child care setting (if child attends more than 10 hours a week). • Telephone interviews with mother every 3 months. Phase II: • At 4 1/2 years old and in grade 1, home visits, lab assessments, child care setting observation, school observation. • During kindergarten, parents and teachers complete mailed questionnaires and phone interviews.	Child care: • quality, • history of enrollment, • type, • stability, • hours. Home environment. Child development: • cognitive, • social, • attachment, • emotional. Mother's development.

Contexts Studied	Planned Linkage Capacities	Incentive Given?	Type of Data Collection	Information Contact (as of 2/98)
Phase I: • child care, • home/family. Phase II: • child care, • home/family, • school.	No linkage.		Phase I: • Face-to-face and telephone interviews. • Videotaping of play/interaction. • Observation of child, parents, primary child care setting, family setting. • Standardized tests/assessments of child development. Phase II: Same as Phase I, with the addition of observation and interviewing of teachers and schools.	Sarah Friedman National Institute of Child Health and Human Development National Institutes of Health 9000 Rockville Pike Bethesda, MD 20892 Phone: (301) 496-9849

TABLE B-1   Continued

Survey	Sample	Oversamples	Planned Periodicity	Major Topics
Panel Study of Income Dynamics (PSID)	National sample of 5,000 households, beginning in 1968. 8,700 households in 1996.	African Americans. Hispanics in 1990-1995, with Cubans and Puerto Ricans oversampled relative to Mexican Americans.	Annual, since 1968.	Family structure, dynamics, and financial status, specifically: • family composition, • demographic events, • income sources and amounts, • employment, • poverty status, • public assistance, • housework time, • housing, • socioeconomic background, • health.
Panel Study of Income Dynamics: Child Development Supplement (CDS)	National sample of 3,500 children 0-12 years old. Includes approximately 550 immigrant children. Also: • 2,500 mothers, • 2,000 other caregivers and noncustodial parents, • 1,415 teachers, • 1,226 school administrators.	African Americans.	Began in 1997. Will follow children into adulthood.	Early human capital formation.

Contexts Studied	Planned Linkage Capacities	Incentive Given?	Type of Data Collection	Information Contact (as of 2/98)
Economics. Demography. Sociological factors. Psychological factors. Family unit. Primary adult. Family members. Neighborhood.	Medicare records. National Death Index (NDI), Panel Study of Income Dynamics geocode. Does not have Social Security number links Census data via address.		Interviews of family members.	Sandra Hofferth Institute of Social Research University of Michigan 426 Thompson St. Room 3234 Ann Arbor, MI 48106 Phone: (313) 763-5131 E-mail: Hofferth@umich.edu Website: www.umich.edu/-psid
Cognitive development. Socioemotional well-being. Health. Parents/family. Neighborhood. Teachers. Schools. Time use.	Census Bureau information on neighborhoods.		Initial in-home interview of family members. Telephone interviews of family members. Woodcock Johnson achievement test. Self-administered questionnaires completed by child's teacher and school or child care provider.	Sandra Hofferth Institute of Social Research University of Michigan 426 Thompson St. Room 3234 Ann Arbor, MI 48106 Phone: (313) 763-5131 E-mail: Hofferth@umich.edu Website: www.umich.edu/-psid

TABLE B-1   Continued

Survey	Sample	Oversamples	Planned Periodicity	Major Topics
Program of Research on the Causes and Correlates of Delinquency Three coordinated projects: • Denver Youth Survey, • Pittsburgh Youth Study, • Rochester Youth Development Study.	Probability sample of 4,544 inner-city youth, ages 7-15 in 1987. Denver: (N = 1,527) 7, 9, 11, 13, 15 year olds in 1987 living in stratified sample of households. Pittsburgh. (N = 1,517) First, fourth, and seventh graders attending public schools in 1988. Rochester: (N = 1000), 7th and 8th graders attending public schools in 1998.	Youth at high risk for serious delinquency (all three states).	Denver: Annual interviews; 1988-1992, 1994-1999. Pittsburgh: Youngest and oldest cohorts—every 6 months, 1988-1991; annually,1994-1999. Middle cohort—every 6 months, 1988-1991. Rochester: Every six months, 1988-1992; annually, 1994-1997. Potential continuation through 2002.	Delinquency. Violent behavior. Drug use/abuse. Gang membership. Psychopathology. Victimization. Employment. Sexual behavior and pregnancy. Use of mental health services.

Contexts Studied	Planned Linkage Capacities	Incentive Given?	Type of Data Collection	Information Contact (as of 2/98)
Individual. Peer. Family and parenting. Schools. Neighborhood opportunities and social disorganization.	Common measures and analyses three states. Common measures and collaborative analyses possible and in progress with other longitudinal research projects.	Monetary or merchandise incentives across all youth and parent respondents.	Face-to-face interviews in private settings with youth provided to caretakers. Archival data from police, courts, schools, social services.	Program information: David Huizinga Institute of Behavioral and primary Science University of Colorado Phone: (303) 492-1266 Denver study: David Huizinga (see above) Pittsburgh study: Rolf Loeber Life History Studies University of Pittsburgh Phone: (412) 383-1015 Rochester Study: Terrence Thornberry School of Criminal Justice University of Albany Phone: (518) 442-5218

TABLE B-1   Continued

Survey	Sample	Oversamples	Planned Periodicity	Major Topics
Project on Human Development in Chicago Neighborhoods (PHDCN) Two studies in one: • Community survey (CS) • Longitudinal cohort study (LCS)	1. CS: Split Chicago into 343 neighborhood clusters (NCs) using 1990 Census data. All clusters were in the sample for CS. Target number of interviews to complete = 9,260 (interview one person 18+ years old in each chosen household). 2. LCS: 7,000 children and youth (ages prenatal to 18) and their families from 80 randomly selected, representative NCs. • Seven cohorts of 1,000 each (0-1, 3, 6, 9, 12, 15, and 18 year olds in 1996). • 50% male/50% female. • Balanced representation of African American, Latino, white, and mixed communities. • Three socio-economic levels based on income. • Includes children from all social classes in each ethnic group. (Added in 1994) Infant Study: 400 infants, ages 5-7 months	None.	1. CS: Completed in 1996. 2. LCS: Study will cover 8-year period from 1995-2003. • Uses "accelerated longitudinal design"—nine different age groups (from ages 0 to 18) will be followed over the 8 years. • Annual interviews.	How social and physical environments affect human development, specifically origin and development of social competence vs. antisocial behavior.

Contexts Studied	Planned Linkage Capacities	Incentive Given?	Type of Data Collection	Information Contact (as of 2/98)
Community. Neighborhood. Family. Peers. Individual characteristics. Schools.		$30 incentive payment is given. As an added incentive, participants' names are entered in a monthly lottery of $100.	1. CS: • Interviews with households and key community members. • Systematic observations of the communities' physical and social characteristics. • Official records. 2. LCS: • Field interviews with individuals using computer (in English, Spanish, and Polish).	Stephen Buka Harvard School of Public Health 677 Huntington Ave. Boston, MA 02115-6028 Phone: (617) 432-3870

TABLE B-1   Continued

Survey	Sample	Oversamples	Planned Periodicity	Major Topics
Survey of Program Dynamics for Assessing Welfare Reform (SPD)

Three components:
• 1992 and 1993 SIPP (1992-1996)
• SPI) Bridge Survey (1997)
• SPD surveys (1998-2002) | 35,000 respondents from 1992-1993 Survey of Income and Program Participation (SIPP).

Bridge Survey: 30,000 successful interviews.

1998 SPD: Expects to include approximately 18,500 households. | 1998 SPD: all households under 150% of poverty level and all households with children under 200% poverty level will be included; others will be subsampled. | Data collected will cover a 10-year period that includes pre- and post-welfare reform.
• SIPP 1992: covers 1992, 1993, and 1994.
• SIPP 1993: covers 1993, 1994, and 1995.
• Bridge Survey: covers 1996 (and will get some information from SIPP 1992 participants about 1995); conducted from April to June 1997.
• 1998 SPD: covers 1997; conducted from April to June 1998.
• 1999 SPD: covers 1998; conducted in spring 1999.
• Until 2002, SPD will be administered every spring. | Dynamics of income and program participation, child well-being, evaluation of welfare reform. |

Contexts Studied	Planned Linkage Capacities	Incentive Given?	Type of Data Collection	Information Contact (as of 2/98)
Economics. Social characteristics. Household characteristics. Program participation. Eligibility and money income. In-kind benefits and services received from programs, employment, earned-income, and income from other sources. Family composition. Child well-being and environment.	Social Security number will allow links to earnings records; contextual information on welfare programs in sample counties being collected by Univ. of Wisconsin.	$20 incentive payment given to a sample of low-income respondents in 1997.	In-person and computer-assisted personal interviews (CAPI). Self-administered adolescent survey. Surveys done in Spanish and English. Will conduct a reinterview.	Michael McMahon SPD Operations Manager Demographic Surveys Division Washington, DC 20233-8400 Phone: (301) 457-3819 Fax: (301) 457-2306 E-mail: Michael.F. McMahon@census.gov Daniel H. Weinberg Principal Investigator Housing and Household Economics Statistics Division U.S. Bureau of the Census Washington, DC 20233-8500 Phone: (301) 457-3234 Fax: (301) 457-3248 E-mail: Daniel.H. Weinberg@census.gov

TABLE B-1   Continued

Survey	Sample	Oversamples	Planned Periodicity	Major Topics
Wisconsin Longitudinal Study	10,317 women and men who graduated from Wisconsin high schools in 1957. Sample has been supplemented with all twins and with a randomly selected brother or sister of approximately 5,000 graduates.	No oversamples, excepting a small number of twin pairs.	Data have been collected irregularly and at relatively long intervals from graduates (spring 1957), parents of graduates (1964), graduates (1975), 2,000 siblings (1977), graduates (1992-93), and 5,000 siblings (1993-94). Next planned contact will be in 2000 or 2001.	Effects of social background, ability, and aspirations on post-secondary schooling, occupational standing, and earnings; family formation; sibling resemblance; and health, especially women's health.

Contexts Studied	Planned Linkage Capacities	Incentive Given?	Type of Data Collection	Information Contact (as of 2/98)
Families (including parents, siblings, and children of graduates), schools and colleges, communities, employers.	Data have been linked to selected high school records of graduates and siblings, Wisconsin state tax records of parents, Social Security earnings (of men only), Census geography, college and employer characteristics. Social Security numbers and other identifiers provide a link to the National Death Index for parents, graduates, and siblings, and offer possible future linkages to OASDI and Medicare records.	No tangible incentives have ever been offered, except to a very small subsample now participating in a small biomedical study.	Surveys of graduates, parents, and siblings by telephone and mail. More than 85 percent of survivors of the original cohort of graduates participated in the 1992-93 telephone interview.	Robert M. Hauser (hauser@ssc.wisc.edu), Vilas Research Professor of Sociology University of Wisconsin-Madison, 1180 Observatory Drive Madison, WI 53706 E-mail to wls@ssc.wisc.edu. Documentation and public data files are available at: http://dpls.dacc.wisc.edu/WLS/.

APPENDIX
C

Workshop Agenda

WORKSHOP ON LONGITUDINAL SURVEYS OF CHILDREN

National Research Council
Washington, D.C.
September 12-13, 1997

Friday, September 12

9:00 a.m. Welcome and Introduction

Barbara Boyle Torrey, *Executive Director, Commission on Behavioral and Social Sciences and Education*
Robert Hauser, *Workshop Chair, University of Wisconsin*
Jeremy Travis, *Director, National Institute of Justice*

9:30 *Session 1:* Introduction to the Surveys

What data are we collecting on children and how? Each survey representative will be asked to make a brief presentation of five minutes or less to summarize the goals, purposes, and central substantive issues that guided development of the study; the overall design, the sampling strategy, the constructs being assessed, and the measurement instruments, as well as the current status of the survey. These presentations will rely heavily on summary materials that were collected from each presenter prior to the workshop and distributed to all workshop participants.

10:45 Break

11:00   *Session 2:* Major Conceptual and Methodological
             Survey Challenges: Experiences and Best Strategies

             *Each survey representative will identify one or two challenges they
             faced regarding design, measurement, or methodology. These will
             serve as the focal points for the session. The survey representatives
             will be asked to spend a few minutes on the issues they identified.
             Discussion will ensue with the entire group, so that all concerns
             can be addressed and solutions shared. Ample time has been allot-
             ted for this session in order to cover all issues.*

             Examples of potential issues/challenges:

             • Coverage and balance of content.
             • Sampling design and weighting.
             • Measurement and analysis.
             • Field operations.
             • Legitimation and retention of cases.
             • Data disclosure and dissemination.
             • Overall resources for longitudinal (and other) studies.

12:30 p.m.   Lunch

1:30   Continue discussion of Session 2

3:00   Break

3:15   Continue discussion of Session 2

5:30   Adjourn

Saturday, September 13

9:00 a.m.   *Session 3:* Conceptual Issues Facing Surveys in Today's Policy
             and Community Context

             *This session is designed to provide presenters with the opportunity
             to brainstorm to identify important trends for children and future
             policy issues that might affect children and how current and future
             data could meet the needs for informing those policies.*

Some issues for discussion:

- Measurement of family economics: Patterns of receipt of public assistance, fluctuations in and sources of family income, assets.
- Measurement of community/neighborhood context.
- Capacity to inform efforts to trace implementation and effects of devolution: How to assess policy/community context? What effects to look for?
- Continuity of care.

10:45   Coffee Break

11:00   Continue discussion of Session 3

12:30 p.m.   Lunch

1:30   *Session 4:* Collaboration

             Each presenter will be asked to suggest further ways in which collaboration could be fostered among all principal investigators of longitudinal surveys of children and to discuss the sharing of research protocols, data linkages, and archiving of data.

2:30   Summing up: What Have We Learned?

3:00   Adjourn